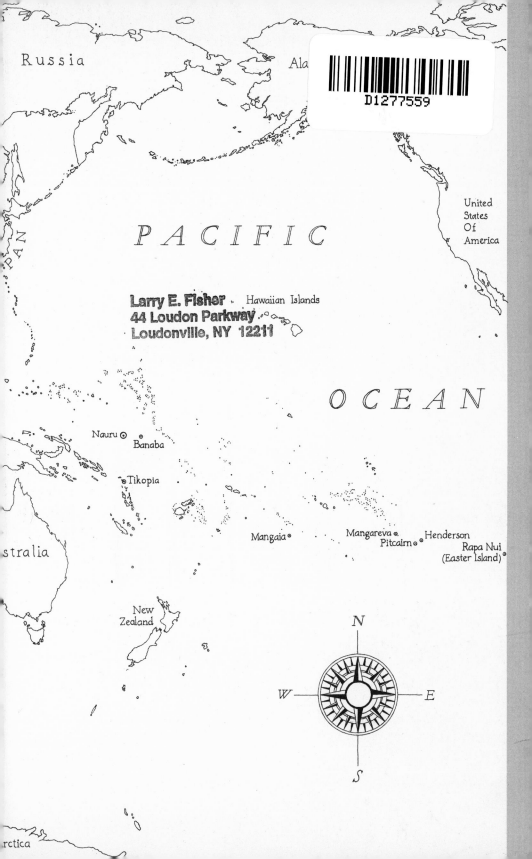

Russia

Ala

D1277559

United
States
Of
America

PACIFIC

OCEAN

Larry E. Fisher · Hawaiian Islands
44 Loudon Parkway
Loudonville, NY 12211

Nauru ⊙ ●
Banaba

Tikopia

Mangaia ●

Mangareva ●
Pitcairn ●

Henderson
Rapa Nui
(Easter Island) ●

stralia

New
Zealand

N

W ● E

S

rctica

Carl N. McDaniel
and John M. Gowdy

Paradise for Sale

A PARABLE OF NATURE

UNIVERSITY OF CALIFORNIA PRESS

Berkeley   Los Angeles   London

University of California Press
Berkeley and Los Angeles, California

University of California Press, Ltd.
London, England

© 2000 by Carl N. McDaniel and John M. Gowdy
Illustrations © 2000 by Abigail Rorer

Library of Congress Cataloging-in-Publication Data
McDaniel, Carl N., 1942 – .
  Paradise for sale : a parable of nature / Carl N. McDaniel and
John M. Gowdy.
    p.   cm.
  Includes bibliographical references and index.
  ISBN 0-520-21864-7 (cloth : alk. paper)
  ISBN 0-520-22229-6 (pbk. : alk. paper)
  1. Sustainable development—Nauru. 2. Environmental
economics—Nauru. I. Gowdy, John M. II. Title.
  HC682.25.Z9M33   2000
  333.7'099685—dc21   99-12829
                                                        CIP

Manufactured in the United States of America

08 07 06 05 04 03 02 01 00 99
10 9 8 7 6 5 4 3 2 1

The paper used in this publication is both acid-free and totally chlo-
rine-free (TCF). It meets the minimum requirements of American
Standard for Information Sciences—Permanence of Paper for
Printed Library Materials, ANSI Z39.48-1984. ∞

To the people of Nauru
and those of all of the other cultures,
who have enabled us to imagine
a different world

In amnesiac revery it is also easy to overlook the services that ecosystems provide humanity. They enrich the soil and create the very air we breathe. Without these amenities, the remaining tenure of the human race would be nasty and brief.

EDWARD O. WILSON, *The Diversity of Life*

Contents

Illustrations

Acknowledgments

This book has been decades in the making. For most of our professional careers, stretching back more than three decades, we have been hearing and thinking about the ideas that we discuss here. Although it is impossible to know where many of these ideas come from or exactly why we understand them the way we do, we are deeply indebted to all who have been a part of our imprinted but often unremembered histories.

We thank Laura Hartnett for ferreting out materials on Nauru, and we also thank the many people who have read parts of this book, or entire drafts, giving us important and valuable assistance, including: Jonathan Andleson, Susan Blandy, David Borton, Harriet Borton, Steve Breyman, Joe Brown, Kathy Conroy, P. Thomas Carroll, Marti Crouch, Jonathan Erickson, Robert Frazier, Jackie Fleming, Jeff Gersh, Jeff Glikes, Rose Glikes, Keith Harrison, Wes Jackson, Stuart McDaniel, Virginia McDaniel, Bill McKibben, George Mercier, David Orr, Bruce Piasecki, Doug Reed, George Robinson, Harry Roy, Sharon Roy, John Schumacher, Bruce Watson, John Wimbush, and Langdon Winner.

We also wish to express our appreciation to the Nauruan government for allowing us to visit Nauru and personally connect, in some small way, with both its people and the island itself. We thank all of the Nauruans who warmly welcomed us and allowed us to experience firsthand their generous nature and unique pattern of habitation.

We are especially indebted to G. Doyle Daves and Donald Frazier, who believed in us absolutely and commented on all three major drafts, as well as on numerous pieces along the way. We cannot give enough credit to Doyle for his unfaltering criticism of the unbelievable — he held our feet to the fire until we told the truth.

We give our special thanks to Edward O. Wilson, who read a draft and introduced us to Howard Boyer, who immediately saw the promise in our rough-hewn stone. The carving and polishing were accomplished under Howard's masterful guidance, and Rachel Berchten's superb editorial skills completed the job. Howard also introduced us to Abigail Rorer, whose exquisite illustrations capture meaning and add beauty. Our wives, Mary and Linda, have our unconditional appreciation for they have endured much but never failed in their support.

Creating a book is like running a marathon. The event itself — running the 26 miles 385 yards — is intense but merely a several-hour passage, whereas the thousands of preparatory miles in good and bad weather, in health and sickness or injury, and the wondering "why?" are deeply imprinted in one's being. The bonding and support of many make running the marathon possible, but in the end, the event belongs to the runner. And so it has been with this book. The people mentioned above, and others, have done their best to help us do it right, but in the end we accept responsibility for what we have written.

Paradise for Sale

Prelude

OUT OF THE AIRPLANE window I had seen nothing but azure ocean in every direction for hours. The FASTEN SAFETY BELT sign flashed on and we were instructed to prepare for landing. As the 737 banked into its glide path, I could clearly see the devastation on the small island below. For years my friend and colleague Carl McDaniel and I have been interested in the history of other cultures, especially in the many examples of "overshoot and collapse" that seem typical of complex human societies that emerged since the advent of agriculture. Just a year earlier I had walked into Carl's laboratory and said, "Here it is! Our Easter Island," as I handed him a short article in the *New York Times* titled "A Pacific Island Nation Is Stripped of Everything."

Carl and I had been writing scholarly papers together for several years and the current project was a general audience book highlighting the conflict between biological diversity preservation and the expanding commercial economy. Nauru appeared to symbolize the fate of the planet — my wife, Linda, and I were going to check it out. Our Air Nauru flight from Brisbane, Australia, had been delayed and then canceled until the next day. Rumors were flying: "The President needed the plane to fly in shrimp for a big party he was throwing," or "A key part was missing, and no one was bothering to look for a replacement." The preconceived notions of people from the industrialized world about native people in general and about Nauruans in particular led to quick explanations of Air Nauru's difficulties — avarice and sloth. After an hour or so we talked to the wife of an Air Nauru pilot and learned that the plane had been delayed because of difficulties with an airport landing system in New Zealand. We departed the next morning on schedule.

It was Christmas Eve on Nauru. The road from the airport to the Menen Hotel was crowded with cars full of people singing and laughing on their way to the season's festivities. We were surprised at how happy the people were. I suppose we naively expected them to be in a constant state of depression about the destruction of their homeland and their bleak prospects. We checked into the Menen Hotel situated in a residential area on the eastern side of the island. Our guidebook had told us to expect the service to be poor to nonexistent. "If it looks like there's nobody on duty at the reception desk, look behind the counter: the clerk may be asleep on the floor." That Menen was gone; at this new Menen Hotel, the service was efficient, pleasant and professional. The building itself was new and elegant, with spectacular views of the reef and the ocean beyond. We tossed our bags into our room and started walking to stretch our legs after the long plane ride. Although we had spent the previous week hiking in Australia, we were unprepared for the stifling heat of Nauru. Hardly a breeze stirred as we passed the water trucks making deliveries to the hotel and headed for the commercial district along the paved road that circled the island. Having read several articles about "the richest island in the Pacific," we were surprised to find that all the houses we saw, although certainly comfortable and adequate for the tropical climate, were modest. We passed several small restaurants, a school, and a cemetery, where we noted the early age of death on many tombstones. We walked through the commercial center, then turned inland on a road that passed the phosphate processing facility. At the top of the hill we turned right onto a dirt road that headed into the mining area on the central plateau of the island called Topside.

We passed areas that had been mined decades ago and were surprised to see how much the vegetation had reestablished itself — life had recolonized the debris and coral pinnacles that remained after the phosphate ore had been removed. Small trees grew at improbable angles from the nooks and crannies of the coral outcrops. Vines, ferns, grasses, small bushes and sizable trees now filled what had been a wasteland. In the heat the verdant smell of thriving vegetation was refreshing. Birds sang and flew in areas now inaccessible to humans, while small animals scurried about in the brush.

The sides of the road were sprinkled with beer and Spam cans and assorted remnants of the technological civilization that had been imported to Nauru — wheels, pulleys, cable, shards of glass, plastic, and myriad forms of twisted, bent, and rusting iron. At some places along the road beer cans were strewn several meters apart, while at others they were piled in blue heaps of Fosters or green mounds of Victoria Bitter. We had seen signs urging people not to litter and to recycle. Despite the litter, we also saw much recycling — piles of crushed and neatly bundled cans along the side of a large building. Just beyond this recycling area was Nauru's landfill. Surprisingly, a truck drove past us into the dump and sounds of heavy machinery in the distance told us that Christmas Eve was a regular work day for some.

Oddly, the breeze one might expect on such a small island was absent that day. As we walked the heat became more and more oppressive, the dust from the road annoying, and, occasionally, the stench of garbage was heavy in the air. As we walked further along the desolate road, we came to an area recently mined. This was a truly depressing site but one that irrefutably confirmed our expectations. Bare coral pinnacles, devoid of green regrowth, jutted out as far as the eye could see. In the distance we saw the deep blue of the central Pacific, a beautiful sight that contrasted sharply with the ugly barren moonscape of Topside. We tried to imagine what the area must have looked like before mining: tomano, pandanus, coconut, and almond trees swaying gently in equatorial breezes, birds flying overhead, and insects humming in the tropical heat.

We thought back to the *New York Times* article that had brought us to this stifling-hot wasteland of human creation. According to the *Times'* account, Nauru's experiment with global capitalism had left its land ravaged and its culture in tatters. Most of the land — rich in phosphate — had been dug up and sold overseas; its people had succumbed to the worst excesses of western-style consumption. The Reverend James Aingimea, the eighty-four-year-old minister of the Nauru Congregational Church, lamented, "I wish we'd never discovered that phosphate. I wish Nauru could be like it was before. When I was a boy, it was so beautiful. There were trees. It was green everywhere, and we could eat the fresh coconuts and breadfruit. Now I see what has happened here, and I want to cry." After a hundred years of western occupation, "our cultural traditions have been basically wiped out," said Maggie Jacob, a Nauruan schoolteacher.

Although the phosphate had generated annual profits of tens of millions of dollars for decades, it was unclear how much money remained to provide for the Nauruans now that the phosphate was nearly gone. The government releases no financial data, but the *New York Times* article mentioned failed investments — $12 million ($US) or more lost in an investment scam perpetrated by eight Americans; another $12 million ($US) lost in bogus letters of credit and bankotes purchased on the advice of a lawyer from one of Australia's most respected law firms; $2 million ($US) in an unsuccessful London musical — and questioned how much, if anything, was left in the Trust Funds set aside over decades for the time when the phosphate would be gone. The huge flow of cash through the island allowed Nauruans to live well without working and changed their diet from fish and fruits to one of Spam, potato chips, canned corned beef, and beer. As a consequence Nauruans are obese and have one of the highest rates of diabetes in the world.

On the surface, what we saw confirmed what was written in the *New*

York Times article. Physically the island was a wreck, obesity among the populace was common, and prosperity was obvious — a beautiful hotel, modern houses, and Land Rovers, vans, sport-utility vehicles, motorcycles, and motorbikes everywhere. But, in contrast to what we had read in the article, people appeared happy and went about their business as if there were no crisis. An old Nauruan saying "Tomorrow will take care of itself" alluded to an underlying belief that might explain the behavior we observed. At the same time, this seemed curious to me. After all, on this tiny island of just 21 square kilometers, the devastation jumps out at you! Old people like James Aingimea see and bemoan what has happened to the island and its culture, yet the mining and its destructive consequences are still tolerated if not embraced.

At first glance Nauru is just another very clear-cut case of short-sighted misjudgment that could have been easily avoided. Like the entire planet, Nauru's fate was sealed by greed, corruption, and short-sightedness. The problem and its solution seem obvious: When we realize the folly of both our devastation of ecosystems and our ravenous consumption of the resources that permit human habitation, we will readily change our behavior and will be on the road to sustainability. But, in reality, folly holds the upper hand. Why this is so, as well as why Nauru is a window through which one can see global trajectories into disaster, are the stories we seek to tell.

The more Carl and I had read about Nauru, the more we realized that it was not the exception portrayed by the *Times* article but rather the rule. The story of Nauru is the story of all of us. Phosphate mining on Nauru provides a perfect parable for what our market system is doing to earth. The first humans came to Nauru more than 2,000 years ago and over time created a sustainable culture with a language and a pattern of living found nowhere else. In 1798 a Western whaler happened upon Nauru, and the ship's captain named it Pleasant Island. Extensive coconut groves fueled copra trading, and Germany brought Nauru into the sphere of Western influence. The discovery of one of the richest phosphate deposits in the world placed Nauru onto the global stage. During the first sixty years of phosphate mining, Nauruan culture was engulfed by the West: Christianity, World War I, League of Nations Trusteeship, World War II, deportation under Japanese occupation, and United Nations Trusteeship. By the time independence came in 1968, the tremendous financial wealth from phosphate mining had done its deed — a radically altered Nauruan culture, seduced by the promises of phenomenal monetary wealth, entered a global market economy that has no long-term capacity to ensure human well-being or to foster enduring habitation. In a mere century the island home of this once self-sufficient culture has been transformed into a wasteland of mined-out ruins devoid of much of its initial biological diversity — the 10,000 inhabitants are absolutely dependent upon the outside world for their very survival. Nauru exquisitely illuminates the ruinous course of our global market culture.

Planning for the future does not seem to be a dominant human trait. Pre-agricultural societies are distinguished by their live-for-today mentality. In fact the traditional Nauruan saying about tomorrow taking care of itself has been true — for most of Nauruan history tomorrow did take care of itself. One of the many ironies of modern Nauru is that, under the influence of Western notions of resource exploitation, the destruction of the island provides for today, while future habitability is sacrificed. It appeared to Linda and me, as casual observers, that Nauruans seemed to be unconcerned about their bleak prospects. This raised perhaps the most disturbing question of the trip. If people in such an obviously desperate situation, caused by resource exploitation to the point of almost complete destruction of their natural environment, were unconcerned, what hope is there to convince the rest of the world to be concerned about the more subtle but equally destructive activities going on around them?

Numerous writers and scientists have made the case convincingly clear — the global market system of our technological culture has permitted explosive growth of population and consumption that is unsustainable. Human activities are radically changing the land, the sea, and the air — all of which are causing the sixth mass extinction of biological diversity in the last 600 million years. Our civilization is destroying what makes human existence possible. And our cultural response is more of the same. Why?

For quite a while Carl and I have been struggling with this question. Paul and Anne Ehrlich established in *Betrayal of Science and Reason* what is and is not known about critical and contentious environmental issues. The Ehrlichs use sound logic and established science to counter the arguments of those who, knowingly or unknowingly, have employed incomplete or incorrect information to obfuscate the truly immense challenges before us, including overpopulation, limited food and nonliving resources, threats to biological diversity, changes to atmosphere and climate, and the ubiquity of toxic substances. A reviewer of the book stated that "the Ehrlichs are fighting the smoke, not the fire." This assertion startled us. Suddenly, we realized why both our culture and Nauru's have failed to respond to the crises so well documented by the Ehrlichs. All of the facts, all of the logic, and all of the science are important and necessary, but ultimately insufficient. The fire — our beliefs and their undergirding myths — is the navigator that establishes the course. A culture is driven by the integrated sum of its stories, beliefs, values, ethics, behaviors, and actions. To intellectually assess that one's culture is courting monumental disaster is one thing. It is a wholly different proposition to change our culture's course, but this is the task before us.

The successes of the global market economy are impressive — more people have more things and a higher standard of living than ever before. People in the industrial world are living longer and benefiting from a cornucopia of technological innovations brought forth by the explosion of scientific knowledge in the last several centuries. At the same time, the natural and social sciences are also delivering another message — the current pattern and magnitude of human habitation will be short lived. This abstract message is not reinforced by overt short-term negative feedback signals that might elicit immediate corrective actions. Understanding the message is extremely difficult for most modern-day human beings because we have physically and emotionally extracted ourselves from the larger biological world upon which we utterly depend for our very existence. As a result we are unaware of the dire consequences of the mass biological extinction we are causing. Commentators have noted that the inhabitants of Easter Island, Sumer, and the Mayan Empire, to cite a few of many examples, would hardly have noticed from one generation to the next the biological impoverishment that eventually led to the collapse of their complex societies. How can you miss what you haven't seen? Do residents of North America miss the endless old growth forests filled with an abundance of animals on the ground and birds in the air that greeted the first European explorers? Were the pre-European native North Americans aware of the absence of plains camels, giant armadillos, anteaters, sloths, and mammoths that were here when the first humans arrived over 10,000 years ago?

Linda and I were surprised on Nauru by the resilience of nature as plants and animals recolonized Topside. But this merely confirms what careful observers have written about the consequences of human activities. It is arrogant for us to think that we are "destroying the planet" — Earth got along quite well before humans appeared and will get along quite well after we are gone. Humans may be impoverishing biological diversity by changing the climate and destroying habitat, but the earth's biological diversity has been hammered like this before and it has always bounced back in 10 or 20 million years. Much of the environmental havoc we are wreaking on the planet is certainly reversible, but the time required would render this recovery meaningless to us — humans just won't be here to see it.

Nauru is a story of power, exploitation, greed, and the selling of the future for short-term gain. It is the story of our own past, as well as what might very well turn out to be our future. The Nauruans learned from westerners the global market game and then played their hand. This tragic tale provides a window through which to see our culture's fire blaze its course. Nauru and a host of other cultural stories scattered around the globe render intelligible the numerous fallacies in our cultural beliefs and the trajectories they produce. The extrapolations of these trajectories, enlightened by the perspectives of the natural sciences, predict catastrophe. These revelations and myriad others — we hope — will be sufficient to call forth a new worldview that will elicit dramatic adjustments to our pattern of habitation. Otherwise, we will sear civilization to the bone and turn its bones to ashes.

Chapter One

A Pleasant Island

MILLIONS OF YEARS AGO an isolated volcanic mountain began to push toward the water's surface in the central Pacific. Eventually it reached the light just below the ocean's surface, and the summit was colonized by coral — and thus an island was created. With the comings and goings of ice ages on the northern continents, sea level repeatedly fell and rose, exposing and then submerging the coral pinnacles that constituted the only land for hundreds of kilometers. The island, which would be named Nauru, became a haven for innumerable seabirds. Over eons the bird droppings, or guano, filled the coral canyons and mixed with marine deposits as the island was submerged and resurrected again and again. Beneath the island's surface, the combined efforts of geology and chemistry created from guano and marine organisms an exceptionally rich deposit of what many soils elsewhere lacked: phosphate. Now, nearly all of the phosphate is gone, and the sun bakes the exposed coral skeletons at temperatures inhospitable for most life.

Nauru is just south of the equator, halfway between Hawaii and Australia. With a circumference under 20 kilometers, saucer-shaped Nauru is bordered by a narrow strip of almost infertile land several hundred meters wide. Overlooking this band is a plateau that once supported a panoply of plants and animals. The first humans who arrived there several thousand years ago, probably Micronesians, transformed, and were transformed by, this modestly endowed island. The absence of nearby islands and the strong, westerly flowing equatorial current prevented the Nauruans from becoming seafarers. Their isolation for millennia gave rise to a unique people who spoke a language unintelligible to other Pacific islanders. In the absence of trade or other contact with the outside world, the people of Nauru developed a self-contained, durable society. Year in and year out they lived intimately connected to the other inhabitants, real and imagined, that shared their world of palm trees, noddy birds, sand, sea, and sky.

Westerners who first happened upon Nauru in 1798 were so taken by the congenial nature of the inhabitants and by Nauru's beauty that they

Academy members must be voted in, too

Q: How does an actor become a member of the motion picture academy, so they're able to vote for who is nominated and receives Academy Awards?

— Judy Doris, Old Greenwich, Conn.

A: Timely question, with the Oscars coming up March 26. To become a member of any of the academy's 13 branches, which include acting, you must be nominated by two peers in your branch. The academy tell...

NEWS & VIEWS
By Jeannie Williams

This column appear...
Tuesday through...

— Terrie Neil...
Bradley...

A: Yes, Ellen said ton "is going to be th... ther of our child." ... kidder, Ellen, but t... days you never car... I asked Bolton, ... said, "First of al... Anne and E... you believe... me to h... beau...

named it Pleasant Island. Unlike other Pacific islands, Nauru had no sandalwood, bêche-de-mer, pearls, or tortoiseshell to attract the interest of world markets. Even the long arm of Christianity had to wait, for Nauru was remote and small. Westerners had no reason to intrude on the Nauruans' way of life. So for a while after the first encounter, their ancient cultural patterns remained intact — sports, singing, dancing, gossiping, storytelling, and celebrations, interspersed with disputes and rituals of daily life — and continued to bind the islanders together.

On Nauru — true the world over — humans tell stories that become myths as elements of everyday life are woven into a worldview. Myths enable a culture to survive because they validate beliefs, values, and actions that enable a people to adapt to their biological, physical, and social surroundings. Mythic stories in most cultures address similar questions: How did the world come into existence? What is the origin of humans? How are we related to other peoples? The answers to these questions form a culture's creation story which prompts more questions: Why are we here? How should we relate to the spirit world? What is our part in maintaining the order of the universe? How should we live? These stories, and others, are spun together to form an intricate mythological web that guides a people and enriches their lives.

Enduring myths, then, do more than entertain or give aesthetic satisfaction. They impart meaning to natural events, are the source of norms for corrective behavior, and are the motivating force for Herculean endeavors. Myths cannot be labeled as fanciful, fictional, or merely fabricated; they are the heart of a people's identity.

The formative myths of Western culture come from pagan, Hebrew, and Christian stories and thought. Pagan mythology was a collection of heterogeneous and occasionally preposterous tales when Greek philosophers in the fourth and third centuries B.C.E. (before the common era) recast them. Plato, who was concerned with the method and limits of human understanding, devised an overarching philosophical system that remains a pillar of Western culture. In his system the universe issues from a grand architectural design whose elements are dictated by Ideas and Forms. The abstract patterns of the Ideas serve as templates for copies, albeit imperfect, of the abstract Forms. To understand these abstract Ideas requires a grasp of the stable Forms; hence, a political philosopher would consider the qualities and arrangements of an ideal state just as a physicist might consider those of an ideal gas. From such idealist premises Plato and his successors developed a generalized supermyth that met tight logical criteria.

A major element of this new scheme was the Scala Naturae, the Ladder of Nature, or the Great Chain of Being. Aristotle, Plato's student, was as important as his teacher in its formulation. All living species, patterned on unchanging Form: were positioned on the Ladder. The Ladder ascended from the nonliving to the mosses and ferns to flowering plants to worms and clams to humans on the top rung — the Ladder's most perfect occupants.

The Ladder's grand design combined harmoniously the hierarchies that fit socioeconomic arrangements of the ancient Mediterranean world. It became much more persuasive when ingenious Jewish, Christian, and Muslim thinkers adapted it to their monotheistic beliefs. Thus adapted, the Ladder ascended to the supreme and personal God, while humans, created in the divine image, topped the lower section with a mandate to dominate its animals — and the rest of the world below them — in stewardly fashion. A tier of angels was sandwiched between the divine and human rungs of the Ladder. The whole apparatus — represented in myths and art by a host of images, metaphors, or models — depicted the world as a musical concert or a garden, the latter representation harking back to the agricultural life adopted thousands of years earlier.

Plato's idealism was an armchair enterprise whose starting point was the highest level of abstraction. In contrast to this top-down approach, Aristotle was a bottom-up empiricist who concentrated on the function of organs or organisms. He also laid the foundation for the European way of organizing and classifying knowledge, and the Ladder illustrates his talent for taxonomy.

A central division between Plato and Aristotle is that Plato held that we begin life with preexisting ideas, on which we subsequently reflect; Aristotle believed that the mind resembled a blank slate to be inscribed by the data of experience. Without engaging in the still-unanswered questions raised by Plato and Aristotle, we maintain language and culture impose patterns of thinking and acting so habitual and deeply assimilated that they are hardly recognized. These patterns are exempt from our scrutiny because they are so fundamental that few of us have attained the perspective from which it is possible to question these habits of thinking and acting.

Culturally conditioned patterns of thought and action harbor relics of the mythic narratives that underlie them. Every culture has a worldview derived from and embodied in its stories, beliefs, values, ethics, behaviors, and actions. This worldview points a culture in a certain direction and confirms that course of thinking as correct. Very few, if any, of a culture's enshrined views derive from unconstrained analyses of changing information and understandings. Thinking — philosophical, scientific, legal, or religious — is not value free because the thinkers who create it are not culture free. Bias can, of course, be recognized by reflective people; and judgments can be redirected, yet nonadaptive bias is still difficult to detect and correct. The Ladder of Nature is a seminal idea in Western culture, which places heaven above humans and humans above other forms of life on Earth.

In the late sixteenth century, the English lawyer and philosopher Francis Bacon championed the idea that humans should not merely understand but should also improve the world order by experimental intervention and manipulation, a milestone in Western thought. Within a century this perspective led to widespread acceptance of a doctrine of progress that resonated with other cultural beliefs and practices, including male dominance and European prominence. The European male's task was to tame and improve a savage, imperfect world. This period of European world exploration and colonization was a manifestation of the Baconian vision.

By the seventeenth and eighteenth centuries, when Europeans began to move into the Pacific, Western culture had already been forced to consider a powerful idea precipitated by a host of Europeans, most notably Copernicus, Galileo, Kepler, and Newton. This new understanding, whose core was physical science, represented the world as a machine. Its mechanisms operated by mathematical laws rather than, as in the medieval worldview, by purposeful design. Copernicus substituted the sun for the earth as the center of the universe, while Kepler demonstrated that each planet moved in an ellipse, previously considered a geometrically less perfect Form than the circle. Galileo submitted gravitational behavior to mathematical description, and Newton synthesized astronomy, physics, and mathematics into a system that had the qualities of a mechanical clock. The post-Copernican earth was neither the center of the universe nor the center of the solar system — a disruption of the historic alliance between common sense and the accepted worldview. Displacing the earth from the center of creation was a great demotion for both the planet and humankind.

While westerners began to digest the meaning of a heliocentric existence, the Nauruans still believed they were at the center of the world. For them the sea had always existed, as did Ancient Spider, a powerful god who, in the beginning, dwelt in darkness. Originally the heavens and clouds were combined into solid rock, forming a roof pressed flat upon the earth. Then, Ancient Spider sang and tapped on the upper surface of the stone of heaven and entered the interior, a domain where lesser gods dwelt. He called on these lesser gods to help create Nauru. Ancient Spider ordered Rigi, the butterfly god, to fly between the earth and the stone mass that separated the earth and sky. From two stones Ancient Spider formed a man and a woman, who brought forth many children, whereupon Ancient Spider turned the couple back into stones that can still be seen on Nauru.

This Nauruan creation story has been pieced together from meager information from records of ships, traders, beachcombers, and others who visited or lived on Nauru. No written Nauruan records existed. And the westerners who came to Nauru were not interested in mythology and failed to record Nauruan stories in any detail. Only in the 1930s did an anthropologist visit the island; and even then, her observations were limited because she did not speak the native language. As a consequence of the substantial changes wrought by Western intervention, major elements of ancient Nauruan myths, beliefs, and values had been obscured by the time anthropologists sought to record them. Nonetheless, a rough outline of ancient Nauruan culture survives.

Although it occupies about four-fifths of the small island, the central plateau on Nauru called Topside, which rises tens of meters above the thin strip of coastal land, was uninhabited except for periods of building canoes with wood from the tomano tree (*Callophyllum inophyllum*) and the annual pandanus (*Pandanus tectorius*) harvest. People lived only on the coast and in an area around Buada Lagoon, a small brackish inland pond. For about two millennia a population of about one thousand called Nauru home. Most women had only two or three children even though they typically married soon after puberty. Although a taboo against sexual intercourse — beginning after conception and lasting until the child started to walk — reduced birth frequency, drought was perhaps the impetus for maintaining a stable population. Annual rainfall varies dramatically — 28 to 459 centimeters — and periods of low rainfall occur frequently and often last for several years. Because the Nauruans had limited supplies of freshwater and depended on the fruits and sap of coconut and pandanus trees for much of their diet, these dry periods led to intensified prenatal and infant vitamin deficiencies and mortality. In response, Nauruans created a culture adapted to the climate and the biological resources that maintained a stable population for thousands of years.

In all likelihood the first, and subsequent, voyagers had missed their intended destination and been stranded on Nauru, a hospitable island. A mixture of physical types was evident in the varieties in skin

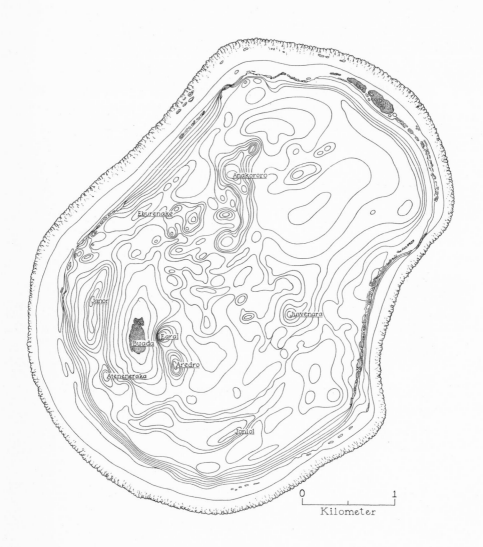

Anakororo

Eburenake

Janor

Buada Earal

Aredro

Ateneneraka

Jonioi

Ciuwenara

0   1
Kilometer

pigmentation, hair, lips, and eye shape found in the Nauruans. Characteristic of Polynesians, they had a tendency to put on fat, a distinct adaptive advantage in times of drought and limited food. In fact, fatness was prized, even considered beautiful. Elements of the Nauruan language point to Micronesian origin, though it is different from other Pacific island tongues. The ancient Nauruans had Micronesian, Melanesian, and Polynesian ancestors, but these forebears had emigrated to Nauru so long ago that Nauruans had their own unique biological and cultural characteristics.

The Nauruans divided themselves into eleven matrilineal clans and established a twelfth clan for foreigners. Myths explained the origin of the matrilineal clans, but the clan evidently was not a ritual unit. The eldest son of the woman who traced her lineage back to the female founder of the clan was the most important male in the clan. The female founders and their lineages were by birth members of the elite class in Nauruan society, the *temonibe*. The middle class, the *ameneñame*, was composed of individuals who generally had substantial amounts of land and other wealth, while the *itsio,* the serf class, were often landless and sometimes the property of a *temonibe*. Class status was not absolutely rigid since wealth could be acquired and *temonibe* designation might be gained through great feats in physical conflicts; marriage above one's class also raised the status of children born of such a union.

Marriage to a member of one's own clan was not permitted, so that a Nauruan might only marry someone from a different clan. *Temonibe* of one clan tended to marry *temonibe* from other clans — with many exceptions, however. After marriage a couple could establish a home with either family or make arrangements to live with or near other relatives. So the members of any single clan became dispersed throughout the island. As a rule, members of the same clan would not fight against each other in disputes that arose between districts or villages. More important, in normal social life persons from the same clan had obligations to each other, especially of hospitality, since social life was centered around clan and family.

Marriage was prohibited not only within a clan but also among close relatives in the clan of one's father. A spouse was secured by betrothal or elopement. When a daughter was born to a *temonibe* woman, a *temonibe* man might tie around the baby's waist a thread from his pandanus-leaf skirt, thereby claiming the daughter for a grandson or another close relative who was also *temonibe*. For other *temonibe* daughters, marriage was arranged before puberty.

Among the rest of the population, marriages came about by a complex ritual that gave each family and the two young people opportunities to assess the partnership. Parents and elder kinsfolk of a boy who had come of age, usually at eighteen, would decide on a mate. A group of young men would indirectly invite the eligible girl to visit the boy's home. Accompanied by another unmarried girl, the young woman would then visit the boy's family for three days, after which the girl's family would visit his family. They would then invite the boy and a male friend to come visit them for three days. These standard formalities were faithfully followed. If the girl's family approved of the marriage, they invited the boy to come live with them. If the boy or his family did not approve, he did not accept the invitation. If he accepted, he got to know the family and gradually came to live with the girl as her recognized spouse. During this period of getting acquainted, the arrangement could be ended by the boy saying he must return home for a while because of his grandmother. His leaving, or termination at other decision points, gave no offense to any of the parties.

Not all marriages were arranged. Sometimes deep passion engulfed a young couple not likely to be united by family and kinfolk. Such a pair might elope and live with a relative. The parents had the right to disown a child who eloped, but family bonds were usually stronger than the anger and disappointment of the moment. In the end, most parents came to accept their children's choices and embraced the new family.

Prior to marriage or betrothal, there was no stigma attached to premarital sex. Indeed, the Nauruans had no word for "virgin." If a girl got pregnant, her family usually asserted their authority and made the couple marry. Extramarital affairs could result in divorce — betrothed and married women were expected to be faithful — but it was not uncommon for amorous relations to lead a man or woman to ask for a spouse's permission to have a second spouse, a request that could not be denied.

Although membership in a clan was established by the mother, the father — not a matrilateral male — was the dominant male in the child's life. In this matrilineal society, when a divorce occurred in a family with children, the children generally would be placed in their father's custody. The extended family was the most significant social group. Children were raised without physical punishment and taught from an early age to value generous giving; as with many Pacific island cultures, no request could be denied. Interestingly, there was no double standard for parents and children — parents always granted their children's requests. Cultural patterns of behavior were not enforced in any formal way. Within the family, a senior member settled disputes or punished deviations from norms. Scorn and public embarrassment encouraged compliance with accepted patterns of behavior, while interclan disputes were settled by what has been called war. Prior to European influence Nauruan weapons were rudimentary, and the images conveyed to us by the word "war" are inappropriate to characterize how interclan disputes were settled on Nauru. In addition, it would be difficult for all members of the feuding clans to separate themselves physically when they lived intermixed on an island of only 21 square kilometers.

The family was the economic unit, but rights to the use of land, trees, fishing areas, sections of Buada Lagoon, and other material goods — as well as those to the use of songs, dances, legends, and designs and ornaments — were controlled by individuals or small groups. Both men and women had rights, although inheritance patterns favored possession of rights and property by women. When a woman died, her property and rights went to her daughters with most of it going to the eldest; when a man died, his property — except canoes, fishing tackle, and weapons, which went to his sons — likewise was inherited by his daughters, with a living wife controlling it until her death, at which time it would revert to the daughters. Men and women retained all of their property rights after marriage and could give away these rights as they chose while they were alive.

The strong equatorial current made extensive deep-sea fishing risky, although in calm weather men did venture in outrigger canoes beyond the reef to catch the prized bonito and yellowtail. They spearfished from the reef and caught flying fish in nets by torchlight. This ocean fishing was carried out exclusively by men and was taboo for women, who were never allowed even to step into a canoe. Speared fish and those caught in traps along the reef were never eaten by women although women could own the rights to the channels in the reef where traps were set. Fish farming provided a reliable source of food when heavy seas curtailed fishing and when droughts depleted fish stocks on the reef. They caught fry of the *ibija* fish (*Chanos chanos*, also called milkfish) in small, flat, coconut-leaf sieves at low tide in reef tidal pools and then raised them in half-coconut shells for several weeks. The salt water was slowly replaced by freshwater, and the acclimated fish were then released into the owner's section of Buada Lagoon or another inland pond. After about a year and a half, when mature, the fish were netted. Although the fish were technically the farmer's property, he had obligations to those who helped catch the fry, the caretaker of his pond, and those who had helped net the mature fish. In addition, a request for some of the harvest could not be denied; thereby, segments of the wider community always participated in the harvest. A man's catch from ocean fishing was treated similarly: the custom of *pwibwi* allowed a man to request from a fisherman a part of his catch, and if the fisherman was a stranger, no obligations were incurred for any kind of return gift.

In the tropical islands of the Pacific, human habitation was almost always associated with the coconut tree. A Nauruan story tells of a time when the islanders became so wicked that the creator punished them by killing all of the coconut palms. This was, indeed, a severe punishment. Wood from the trunk was used for framing their houses and the leaves for roof thatch. An important source of vitamins came from toddy, a

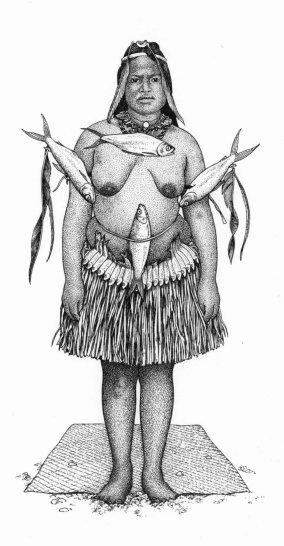

drink prepared from the sap collected from the immature flower bud and consumed fresh. When green, the nuts provided milk, and the meat of the nut could be eaten or stored for times of drought. The dried meat is 50 to 70 percent oil and when extracted was used on the hair and skin. The shell of the nut was used to make household utensils or to carry and raise *ibija* fry before they were released into inland pools. The leaves were fashioned into the traditional foot-long skirt, *ridi*, or woven into mats or baskets. The leaves were also used to create sections in Buada Lagoon for each fish farmer's stock. The fibers that surround the nut and those in the trunk were twisted into cord for weaving fishnets and bird cages, attaching shark-tooth spear blades, tying posts and rafters together, attaching outriggers, binding boat boards together, and other tasks. A Nauruan's wealth and status was a function of the number of tree rights possessed, and when land exchanged hands, the rights to the coconut trees were not automatically included with other land rights.

The Nauruans must have been exceedingly wicked for their creator to kill all of the coconut trees. After a long period of time without coconuts, so the legend tells, a coconut palm sprouted from the grave of a man named Agowénijeng, who was thought to have communicated with the spirits. As a consequence, all coconuts have two eyes, a nose, and are shaped like the skull from which the coconut tree grew.

The screw pine, or pandanus, was perhaps even more valuable than the coconut palm. It begins life as a rosette similar in appearance to a yucca plant, whose sword-shaped leaves display sharp spines on their midribs and edges. Once established, a spiny central stalk grows to a height of about three meters and another cluster of spirally arranged leaves is produced. Aerial roots grow from the trunk and near the top cluster of leaves. When these prop roots reach the ground, they anchor the plant in such a way that it soon appears supported by stilts. Lateral branches grow from the trunk and also form aerial prop roots. The tree can continue to grow in this fashion until it covers a large area. Pandanus leaves, less coarse than coconut leaves, were used for making fine mats and baskets, caulking canoes, thatching roofs, *ridis*, and other things requiring fine fibers. The orange-colored, soccer-ball-size fruit breaks into sections that were chewed for their flavor, or the fibrous fruit was stewed to yield a juice that was made into a palatable black paste. This paste was dried into *edoño*, a thin, flat sheet up to a meter wide and several meters long that was rolled and stored for up to six years. The pandanus harvest and the making of *edoño* began in August or September and took two to three months. Some people moved temporarily onto Topside, where the pandanus grew, because the job was intense and involved the cooperation of many people. The hard work of harvesting and converting the fruits into preserve allowed little relaxation for those involved, but completion was celebrated in a great harvest festival with singers and dancers performing over the island for days.

Most coconut trees were cultivated in the coastal strip or around Buada Lagoon, while pandanus trees grew on Topside and the coast. Although we have scant record of how other species of plants and animals were used in traditional Nauruan culture, it is clear, judging from other subsistence cultures, that many species had specific uses. However, the mainstays of the Nauruan diet were the fish resources of the reef and nearby ocean, along with the fruits and sap of coconut and pandanus trees.

Nauruan life was rich with festivals, singing, dancing, sports, games, storytelling, and just being sociable, mainly because it was easy, except in times of severe drought, to satisfy life's basic needs. The Nauruans had normal disputes, some of which led to clan conflict. Insects and other pests could be annoying. But fish were simple to catch or raise, coconut and pandanus trees essentially grew themselves, and the climate was pretty much the same year round, except for rainy periods. The little work that had to be done was mostly carried out by middle-aged members of the family; women gathered and prepared the food and men fished. The younger people sang, danced, wove mats, wrestled, played ball games, made love, socialized, invented string figures, and enjoyed life.

People in the industrialized world, where consumption is encouraged and progress is presumed, might consider traditional Nauruan life boring and narrow, perhaps even lacking in purpose or meaning. So deeply rooted is our tendency to canonize our own familiar ways that cultural biases, as anthropology teaches, severely impede one's capacity to appreciate or evaluate another culture. What we do know, however, is that prior to the arrival of Europeans more than a hundred generations of Nauruans apparently lived out their lives in relative harmony without a completely disruptive social upheaval or natural disaster. They relied on their enshrined myths and stories to give incentive, direction, and meaning to life and to elicit adaptive responses to the perturbations they did experience. They were transforming the island even as the island was molding them, and the result was a dynamic social and natural order that endured for millennia. Stasis, however, is never permanent even in the isolated nooks and crannies of planet Earth.

Chapter Two

Progress Comes to Nauru

THE BLANKETING OF EUROPEAN influence across the South Seas commenced on November 28, 1520, when the *Concepción,* the *Trinidad,* and the *Victoria* under the command of Ferdinand Magellan sailed into the Pacific Ocean through the strait that now bears his name. Magellan's ships ventured into a vast, uncharted ocean as they sailed up the South American coast and then out across the Pacific Ocean. After six weeks, provisions were exhausted, and crew members began to die. The island of Pukapuka provided water and turtle eggs, but after several more weeks of sailing west all provisions were exhausted. With only old leather, sawdust, and rats to eat, most of the crew became sick with scurvy and starved. More died, and the rest were saved from a similar fate only by eating the fresh fruits and vegetables given them by the natives of Guam in the Marianas. From the east Europeans had entered an immense ocean whose islands had been populated thousands of years earlier by people who sailed from the west. The first Europeans in the Pacific survived because of the generosity and hospitality of the islanders.

Almost three hundred years passed after Magellan's voyage before a Western ship happened upon Nauru. On November 8, 1798, the whaling ship *Hunter* rounded Nauru, and many canoes ventured out to meet the ship. The *Hunter*'s crew did not leave the ship nor did Nauruans board,

but Captain Fearn's positive impression of the island and its people led to its characterization by its English name, Pleasant Island. The Nauruans carried no weapons, and they were not tattooed, as were many other Pacific islanders. Fearn was surprised at how many natives he saw: several hundred in canoes and countless others on the beach. This first encounter was brief and peaceful.

The island's remote location and small size isolated it from European influences for a few more decades. Although Magellan and other explorers opened the Pacific to European influence, Western culture's first emissaries to many of the Pacific islands were beachcombers. They were often deserters from whaling ships or runaway convicts who lived independent lives, sometimes preying upon, and at other times helping, the islanders. Most were transients, but some stayed and adopted an island's traditional way of life. Beachcombers were among the first westerners to transmit the European worldview to Pacific islanders.

The first Europeans to live on Nauru were Patrick Burke and John Jones, Irish convicts who had escaped from Norfolk Island, an English penal colony set aside for the worst criminals transported to Australia.

They were reputed to have been on the *John Bull*, a ship that had mysteriously disappeared in 1830. Several of those who pirated the *John Bull* reportedly ended up on Ponape Island, while Jones and Burke proceeded to Nauru; along the way they ate all of their shipmates. In 1837, when five seamen deserted their whalers to adopt the beachcomber's easy life, they found about eight Europeans already on Nauru. The welcome the newcomers received was not what they had expected.

Jones had become Nauru's first, and last, dictator. When the five seamen landed on the island, Nauruans under Jones's command stripped them of their clothes and possessions. They were permitted to stay only by the sufferance of Jones, who, as they soon learned, had set adrift in a canoe two beachcombers who annoyed him. Beachcombing was not what it was cracked up to be, at least not on Nauru in 1837. At the earliest possible moment, the five would-be beachcombers stowed away on the *Duke of York* en route to Sydney, Australia. In October 1841 Jones poisoned seven beachcombers and shot four others so they would not usurp his power, and then he blamed the Nauruans for the deaths. In return the Nauruans ostracized Jones and banished him to Banaba, Nauru's closest neighbor 300 kilometers due east. Jones tried to return several months later, but the Nauruans would not allow him back. By 1845 only two beachcombers remained on Nauru.

Long before Europeans arrived, other Pacific peoples had moved among the islands, and although some of these newcomers were killed or enslaved, many were welcomed. At first the Pacific islanders viewed the strikingly different physical appearance of Europeans with awe, treating them with deference, but as more westerners arrived and their deeds became known, the islanders realized these foreigners were ordinary humans like themselves. Most of the beachcombers in the Pacific were not as disagreeable as Jones. Many respected the islanders, befriending them and treating their leaders and elders with the respect appropriate to their rank. The beachcombers were sensitive to the local norms of behavior and behaved accordingly, and the natives welcomed beachcombers who were integrated as economic and political assets. The newcomers could repair pistols, muskets, cannons, and an abundance of other articles — axes, knives, scissors, pots — that flowed from the ships to the islands. The beachcombers even served as valuable intermediaries between islanders and Europeans who came to trade.

One of the two beachcombers remaining on Nauru in 1845 was William Harris. He, like Jones, had escaped from the British penal colony on Norfolk Island and arrived in 1842 at the age of twenty-nine. In contrast to Jones, however, and in the beachcomber tradition, Harris assimilated native culture and became an influential intermediary as Nauru came under European influence. He took a Nauruan wife, fathered several children, and was adopted as a Nauruan. He became perhaps the only beachcomber the Nauruans ever fully accepted and trusted.

Over the next decades and into the twentieth century the Nauruans traded pigs and coconuts for steel tools, firearms, alcohol, tobacco, and other products of Western civilization. The islanders had quickly acquired the desire for some of these products, notably firearms. Other desires, however, were created by beachcombers and traders. Tobacco, for example, became a staple as a result of smoking schools where pipes and tobacco were handed out free of charge to generate demand.

Each clan and its leaders regarded the beachcombers as invaluable in negotiating trade agreements with visiting sailors and ship's delegates; and the beachcombers gained great advantage in performing such services. The beachcombers were key agents in bringing Western economic concepts to the islanders. At the outset, goods were exchanged by barter, but as the natives learned that all items had a relative value in marks or pounds or dollars, the concept of money as a medium of exchange became accepted. The social and economic consequences of reducing everything to a single dimension — its market price — were not grasped by the Nauruans, nor by anyone else, for a long time to come.

Copra, dried coconut meat, was a major trade item in the tropical Pacific. It was a natural transition for the Nauruans to shift from preparing dried coconut meat for their own use to making commercial copra, because for thousands of years they had been drying and storing coconut meat for the inevitable droughts. These droughts had been coming to Nauru for millennia as a consequence of extended La Niña events, during which westerly winds persist, thereby preventing the El Niño phase of Southern Oscillation, the periodic warming in the eastern Pacific Ocean that brings heavy rains to Nauru. In good years, when Nauru experienced El Niño–associated rains, a million pounds of copra could be produced for export. In 1886 such a crop was valued at 150,000 German marks on the Hamburg market. On Nauru, as on other islands, beachcomber-traders established themselves as middlemen who processed and exported copra. Although the beachcombers provided valuable services, their presence led to aggressive behavior among the natives. In 1852, in a disputed purchase of a cannon, the Nauruans, encouraged by beachcombers, captured the American brig *Inda,* killed the captain and several of the crew, and then set the ship adrift. Several other purported incidents gave Nauru a bad name. An amicable people started to settle quarrels in ways contrary to their traditional customs. For a number of years ships avoided the island whenever possible.

Traditional life was also disrupted by the introduction of alcohol, a drink absent from ancient Nauru. Although the Nauruans had drunk toddy for millennia, it was always consumed soon after it dripped from the cut coconut flower. In the mid 1800s visitors from the Gilbert Islands came to Banaba and introduced a new way of preparing toddy by letting it ferment for several days. The product, though sour, induced new sensations. The Banaban chiefs quickly recognized the disruptive nature of the new drink and put the Gilbertese back to sea in their canoes. The currents brought them to Nauru, where sour toddy took hold, and many islanders began to get drunk regularly.

Guns and alcohol are a reactive combination, as the Nauruans learned in the 1870s during a festival associated with a marriage. When a heated argument developed over a point of etiquette, one of the guests fired a pistol and accidentally killed a young chief. It was clear that the young chief's death must be avenged. In the past, clan conflicts had often begun over similar unfortunate incidents, only this time every family in every clan had guns. One drunken shooting incident led to another until most islanders were involved. A form of guerrilla warfare broke out; people randomly shot at others or sneaked up on an enemy's house at night and shot at a candle, a match, or anything that moved. Women and children were slaughtered. Unlike past conflicts in which traditional behavior had restored peace, the strife was not resolved.

A squadron of the Royal Navy arrived off Nauru on September 21, 1881, and the flagship approached the island to assess the situation. William Harris, the acculturated beachcomber, boarded the ship, and in the evening the flagship semaphored the rest of the squadron: "A civil war on the island. An escaped convict is king. All hands constantly drunk: no fruit or vegetables to be obtained, nothing but pigs and coconuts. The present island-king wants a missionary. He was evidently hungry."

Six years later, while traveling on the schooner *Buster*, F. J. Moss of Auckland went ashore while copra was being loaded. The Nauruans were friendly and in good humor although most of the boys and all of the men were armed with carbines or repeating rifles. The feud was still raging, but they appeared tired of it. From his conversations with Nauruans, Moss surmised that no one wanted to continue, but no one trusted the others to put down arms. The Nauruans wished that someone would simultaneously disarm them all. During his visit with Moss, Harris told the visitor that two members of his family had already been shot and killed and again expressed a strong desire to have a mission established to bring peace to the island.

During this tumultuous period in Nauruan history, the military and economic power of Europe was expanding because of technological innovations such as steam power and telegraphy. The colonial empires were dividing vast areas of the world among themselves. The huge demands of growing industries for raw materials and the quest for new markets for their manufactured goods fueled the expansionist mentality, even in

Germany, where the general imperialist push for colonies had not been strong. England and Germany, wanting to avert conflicts and to protect their interests, reached an agreement in 1886 that established each country's sphere of influence in the western Pacific. The German trading consortium the Jaluit-Gesellschaft had traders on Nauru who recognized the island's capacity for copra production. As the discussions proceeded, the German negotiators adjusted the original line of demarcation slightly south to include Nauru in the German sphere but left Banaba to the British. The British did not object, thus setting the stage for German control of Nauru.

The decade-long civil war on Nauru had not helped copra production, nor could the traders' safety be assured. Traders and German officials proposed, therefore, that the government take an active hand in ruling Nauru. Nauru came under the German Protectorate on April 16, 1888, and a ban on firearms was declared. On October 1, 1888, the German gunboat SMS *Eber* dropped a landing party of thirty-six men on Nauru. Accompanied by William Harris, the armed marines marched around the island and returned with all twelve chiefs, the white settlers, and the newly arrived Gilbertese missionary. The marines kept the chiefs under house arrest until the next morning, when the annexation ceremony began with the raising of the German flag. The Germans explained how the island was to be administered: There would be peace on Nauru and a ban on firearms was promulgated. The Germans told the chiefs that all weapons and ammunition must be surrendered within twenty-four hours or the chiefs would be taken to prison. By the morning of October 3, 765 guns were turned over with at least 1,000 rounds of ammunition. Nauru's devastating internal feud was over.

The annexation of Nauru by Germany had saved Nauruan society from potential self-destruction by sour toddy and guns, yet at the same time the Nauruans lost all control over their island and their destiny. In a mere fifty-eight years, after millennia of self-sufficiency within the confines of their island home, their world had been rearranged. The rearrangement weakened their myths, beliefs, and values, and would ultimately destroy their land and undermine their culture.

Halfway around the world, roughly coincident with the arrival of Patrick Burke and John Jones on Nauru's beaches, another adventure had begun that would challenge the core of Western culture's worldview. In December 1831 a twenty-two-year-old English naturalist named Charles Darwin commenced a five-year voyage around the world on the HMS *Beagle*. Over the next several decades Darwin would gather and ponder massive evidence to demonstrate that all life on the planet, including humans, had evolved over the eons from common ancestors.

The idea of organic evolution was not new: Darwin's painstaking labor had helped transform a speculative conjecture into observationally substantiated scientific theory. How this evolution occurred depended on thousands of variables, and mounting evidence confirmed the theoretical proposition that evolution was haphazard. When the vast quantities of data and evidence were analyzed and understood, it became difficult to argue that the rungs on the Ladder of Nature represented ascending degrees of perfection, or, more to the point, that humans were God's special creation. Darwin and Alfred Russel Wallace, the cotheorists of evolution by means of natural selection, had established the basic mechanism for the common ancestry of all life on earth. Humans were far from the center of the universe, and their endowments, like those of all other organisms, were chance outcomes of a mechanistic, undirected process. The medieval concept of humans' place in the universe underwent a second great change. The fundamental assumption of Western culture's worldview had been wrong: organisms are constantly changing, and the reality of the biological world demands an equality and unity among all life, including humans.

While Western culture continued to assimilate the deeper meanings of organic evolution, the Nauruans were adjusting to European domination. On the morning of October 3, 1888, after all of the guns and ammunition had been turned over to the Germans, the chiefs were released.

Robert Rasch, a German trader on Nauru, was appointed by the imperial commissioner as temporary official until a permanent official could be found. Later in the day the SMS *Eber*, with its marines and the imperial commissioner on board, sailed away. The permanent official, Christian Johannsen, arrived on May 14, 1889. Activities and events on the island had become the concern of the German government and its trading company partner, the Jaluit-Gesellschaft. The senior members of the clans, or chiefs as Europeans called them, had been displaced by higher authority. A European official had been installed, and the Nauruans accepted his authority to settle disputes, to punish, and to keep the peace.

Things began well on Nauru after the Germans took charge. Twenty-six more rifles and several pistols were handed over to Mr. Johannsen shortly after he arrived. No violence of a serious nature was reported for years — except for the deaths of several Gilbertese in a drift canoe just before Mr. Johannsen's arrival — although dozens of minor disputes over coconut tree rights, land boundaries, and the like were heard and resolved. The consumption of sour toddy dropped substantially and was soon banned, as the importing of alcohol had been earlier. Drunkenness vanished.

With trade in guns, ammunition, and alcohol ended by decree, some Europeans worried because the only major commodity left to trade with the Nauruans was tobacco. Others realized that, with luck, the nascent taste for imported foods like bread, rice, sugar, and flour would grow so the natives would come to depend on these and other Western trade items. The resulting need for money would make them more amenable to entering into labor contracts on and off Nauru. These changes, the Europeans reasoned, would enable the Nauruans to improve their lives and participate in the world beyond their small island.

Government officials, warships, marines, administrators of the companies, and other bureaucrats now provided services that the Nauruans had not needed in their traditional society. It was a new type of social organization that formalized and standardized relations between individuals and groups. Although on the surface it seemed more complex than the traditional system it was replacing, in many ways it was simpler. In the past, barter, group decisions, rights, disputes, and other human interactions were subject first to general customs and then to case-by-case resolution. Each situation had its own complexity, and the traditional system could cope uniquely with each occurrence. The new system was more of a one-size-fits-all approach.

In the overtly structured industrialized world, when someone provides a service or a material good, there is a monetary price to pay. Nauru was now a part of this system; the traders had to pay a tax to conduct business on Nauru, and each islander had to pay a head tax in copra. The head tax was fixed from year to year as a function of the island's copra production. The chief of each clan was responsible for collecting the copra from his people. When it was all collected and delivered, the chief received one-third of the sale value in German marks. There is no record of Nauruan protest to the tax; the Nauruans appeared to believe that the new peace and order were well worth a little coconut meat.

In September 1890 the first census of Nauru was conducted, counting 1,294 Nauruans and 24 Gilbertese missionaries and their families. The ratio of men to women, 574 to 720, reflected the disproportionate number of men killed in the long internal conflict terminated by German occupation. Some officials predicted that the population, now removed from the artificial constraints of violent conflict, would grow rapidly. This was not viewed as a problem but as an opportunity. Although Nauru had missed the era of "blackbirding," or the roundup of natives for the slave trade, because of its remoteness and small size, good labor was in short supply throughout the western Pacific. Europeans judged that Nauruan men and women would make good workers since by all accounts they were strong, friendly, good humored, intelligent, and skilled craftspeople. These expectations were unrealized, since few Nauruans ever left their island permanently.

Although the Nauruans had their own system of rituals and beliefs, they were receptive to new ideas. Christianity was no exception. When the first missionaries from the Gilbert Islands arrived in 1887, out of curiosity a number agreed to be baptized. For several reasons the deeper meaning of the ceremony was lost, not the least being the poor Nauruan-language skills of the Gilbertese. Some missionaries also let personal desires overcome professional purposes, especially when one committed adultery with the wife of a chief, and the missionaries were deported. With the arrival of the Reverend Philip A. Delaporte from the American Board of Commissioners for Foreign Missions in 1899, conversion to Christianity began in earnest.

Nauruans, like many isolated groups of humans, had no knowledge of diseases, except for the nutrient and vitamin deficiencies associated with severe drought. The first indication of disease came in 1864 when Captain Brown of the *Nightingale* reported that some natives suffered from venereal disease. Nauruans were spared from plagues that depopulated several Pacific islands — tuberculosis, influenza, leprosy, and dysentery — until after the turn of the century.

The Germans brought Nauru into their sphere of influence in 1886 because they believed it a fertile island with copra trade value. Though it was true that Nauru had exported annual harvests of over a million pounds of copra — almost half the total production of the Marshall, Brown, and Providence islands — these harvests were in the wet years. Rainfall was unpredictable and droughts were frequent. In the mid to late 1890s several dry years in a row had plunged many of the traders deep in debt. The Jaluit-Gesellschaft tried unsuccessfully to be allowed to remove the administrator to save money. The Pacific economic doldrums for the owners and stockholders of the Jaluit-Gesellschaft were soon to end, however.

In 1896 the cargo officer for the Pacific Islands Company on the *Lady M*, Henry Denson, found on Nauru an odd-looking rock that he believed was a piece of a petrified tree. Although he considered making children's marbles out of the rock, it ended up as a door prop in the company's Sydney office. In 1899 Albert Ellis, an officer with the phosphate section of the Pacific Islands Company, was temporarily transferred to the Sydney office to analyze samples coming from the islands. He noticed the doorstop and thought that it looked like Baker Island phosphate, but Denson told him that it was fossilized wood. His daily encounters with the doorstop, however, kept his original idea alive, and after three months Ellis decided to chip off a piece and test it. It was phosphate ore of the highest quality.

Many soils, such as those in Australia, are deficient in phosphate — a must for successful agriculture. In the commercial world unequal distribution of raw materials means an opportunity to trade and to make money. The livelihood of many companies is built on redistributing resources like phosphate that are unevenly scattered about the globe. The Pacific Islands Company in 1899 needed new supplies of phosphate because sources of high-grade guano were becoming hard to find. Ellis's discovery in Sydney instilled the hope that huge sums of money could be made. But concerns were raised when it was rumored that an enormous deposit of phosphate ore had been discovered on Christmas Island in the Indian Ocean. Bringing to market such a large deposit might enable another company to control the market and thus put the Pacific Islands

Company out of the phosphate business. Unfortunately for the Pacific Islands Company, Nauru, with all of its suspected phosphate, belonged to Germany.

As chance would have it, just to the east of Nauru, Banaba shared Nauru's biological and geological history, and the Pacific Islands Company set its sights on that small island. Industrial and governmental secrecy engulfed transactions between Sydney and London as the Pacific Islands Company conspired to secure the wealth hidden in geochemically processed bird droppings and marine deposits. On May 3, 1900, the natives of Banaba granted the Pacific Islands Company the right to mine all phosphate on the island for 999 years at an annual fee of 50 pounds sterling (British). A year later, the Pacific Islands Company became the Pacific Phosphate Company, and all business except phosphate was abandoned.

Based on his investigative visit in 1900, Albert Ellis reported: "The sight of a lifetime. Material in scores of millions of tons which would make the desert bloom as a rose, would enable hard-working farmers to make a living, and would facilitate the production of wheat, butter and meat for hungry millions for the next hundred years to come." Relying on Ellis's assessment, the newly reorganized company continued to pursue Nauru's phosphate. But the negotiations were convoluted and tricky. Four parties were involved — German and British governments, the Pacific Phosphate Company, and the Jaluit-Gesellschaft — and to further complicate the transactions, the Pacific Phosphate Company did not want the enormous value of the phosphate deposit to be known. Shrewd tactics produced an agreement in 1906 that sanctioned mining of Nauru by the Pacific Phosphate Company. The Jaluit-Gesellschaft's mining rights were transferred to the Pacific Phosphate Company for a cash payment of 2,000 pounds sterling (British), 12,500 pounds sterling (British) worth of shares in the Pacific Phosphate Company, and a royalty payment for every ton exported. Although the Nauruans were not a party to the formal agreements, the Germans, out of a concern for fairness, decided to pay the native landowners a small amount for each ton of rock removed from their land.

In the first year over 11,000 tons of phosphate were shipped to Australia. It was a grand success for all of the Europeans who participated. English and German settlements were constructed on Nauru with flower gardens, coral-lined walks, and a two-story house for the German governor. The antenna of a state-of-the-art wireless station reached 128 meters into the sky.

Despite the fact that the central plateau, Topside, was owned by individual Nauruans, the Pacific Phosphate Company took control of the sale and lease of the phosphate-rich areas. In all of the agreements between those mining Nauru, only two clauses referred to native inhabitants. One required that the mining company give notice of the beginning of operations so measures could be taken to look after the interests of the native people. The other allowed the Jaluit-Gesellschaft to assist the Pacific Phosphate Company in addressing any claims that might be made by natives.

The phosphate deposits below the surface of Topside were nestled among the coral skeletons of the island's creators. As a consequence, mining the phosphate was not easy, and with no harbor or accessible anchorages, offshore loading was a challenge. Chinese and other laborers were brought in as miners because the Nauruans had little interest in organized, for-pay labor. By the time World War I began, 100,000 tons were being shipped annually with a value of $12.50 (Australian) per ton when loaded for transport.

Meanwhile, equally far-reaching changes were affecting other aspects of Nauruan culture. After its poor start in the late 1880s, Christianity was firmly established after the arrival of the Reverend Philip Delaporte and his wife in 1899. They thought that "inappropriate" Nauruan ways needed to be changed so native lives could be improved and Nauruans could learn to live as civilized human beings. Women should not do any heavy work because that was men's work. Old people should not be allowed to go into caves and die, but instead must be given food and kept alive. Sexually suggestive, immoral dances were not to be tolerated and everybody, especially women, should be properly clothed — the Mother

Hubbard dress was deemed appropriate female attire. Although they complied, many Nauruan women, for modesty's sake, also wore the traditional coconut or pandanus leaf *ridis* under their dresses. Many men also wore their *ridis* under their new lava-lavas, two yards of cloth wrapped around, and tucked in, the waist. Aside from modesty, a problem arose because the coconut oil rubbed on the body after physical activity and before sleeping soiled the new attire. Nauruans changed their new clothes infrequently, even sleeping in clothes still wet from fishing trips; and they stopped oiling their bodies as often. Because of these changes in hygiene and the influx of foreigners harboring new diseases, the incidence of tuberculosis and other health problems climbed. Nauru's most devastating epidemic occurred in 1907 when dysentery caused 150 deaths. Western beliefs propelled the Christian newcomers to zealously "improve" a society that had been living successfully for thousands of years in a place the Christians had just "discovered."

Along with phosphate mining and Christianity came a gentle but greater exposure to the price-based market economy of Europeans. With the small amounts of money that came to some Nauruans from phosphate mining operations or the sale of copra, they purchased tobacco, sugar, rice, biscuits, canned salmon, and flour. Some developed a taste for these items, but for the most part they were extras — the island's traditional ways still provided the necessities of life for almost all Nauruans. Hence the market economy took a while to come to the people of Nauru. Even so, the phosphate lying under Topside made Nauru and its European masters immediate participants in world markets.

In 1918 the cartographer's line that had placed Nauru under German rule took on unexpected significance. When Germany lost its Pacific possessions after its defeat in World War I, the islands were entrusted to the victors under the Covenant of the League of Nations. The concept embodied in the covenant acknowledged the rights of dependent peoples, and it imposed responsibilities on the nations entrusted to look after these peoples' interests. Nauru's sister phosphate island, Banaba, was under British rule, not international mandate, so it became the moral duty of the British colonial power to look after the Banabans' interests. As we shall see, moral and legal accountability played out very differently for the peoples of these two islands.

As negotiations began over the displaced territories, the tremendous phosphate wealth of Nauru was coveted by Australia, whose delegates lobbied to annex the island. In the negotiations U.S. President Woodrow Wilson held firmly to his policy of no annexations; this limited the United Kingdom, Australia, and New Zealand to the trusteeship of Nauru. The trustees acquired all the assets and rights of the Pacific Phosphate Company, which were subsequently administered by the British Phosphate Commissioners. The three powers signed the Nauru Island Agreement of 1919, which entitled them to the phosphate of Nauru at cost of production. After all was said and done, about 34 million tons of phosphate — over $300 million (Australian) at world market prices — were mined during their tenure as trustees.

Rosamond Rhone from *National Geographic* visited Nauru in 1921 and wrote an article titled "Nauru, the Richest Island in the South Seas." The article describes a native culture that was still vibrant yet a curiosity. The warm, amicable personalities of the people are apparent in the words and pictures. They fish, sing, dance, and practice the traditions of their culture. The word "richest" in the title alludes to phosphate, but the commercial world is still separate from the lives of most of the natives. It is really two cultures coexisting. Like oil and water, they do not mix well, and life goes on. Little progress is made in the 1920s and 1930s to create an independent Nauru, but the Australian farmers have inexpensive phosphate and the Nauruans keep to themselves.

During World War II Nauru fell into Japanese hands. An airstrip was built and the Allies bombed the island. Twelve hundred Nauruans, two-thirds of the native population, were deported to Truk Island, where one out of three died before the war's end. Their traditional culture, already affected by Western patterns of thought and habit, was devastated by Japanese occupation and deportation. On September 14, 1945, the Japanese surrendered to the Australian occupation force, and just over four months later the Nauruans who had survived deportation and forced labor were reunited with their war-torn home.

A new United Nations Trust Agreement was established in late 1947. From a Western perspective life on Nauru returned to normal; the phosphate commissioners again controlled the island's resources. Enormous amounts of money were made by the British Phosphate Commissioners. In 1948 revenues were $745,000 (Australian). A mere 2 percent of this went to Nauruans directly or into their trust funds, and 1 percent was charged for administration. As the years passed, pressures from the Nauruans and from the United Nations Permanent Mandates Commission and the Trusteeship Council led to larger percentages of revenue going to the island's native people. In 1966, two years before independence, the Nauruans were given 22 percent of revenues of just over a million dollars (Australian), while 14 percent went for administration. The British Phosphate Commissioners believed, and maintained, that they were being more than generous since they had no obligation to pay royalties and the Nauruans' needs were more than adequately met. Historical analyses later revealed that the Nauruans held a different opinion.

Neither the League of Nations nor the United Nations ever intended the trusteeships to be permanent. They were temporary arrangements to give the territories under trusteeship time to prepare for independence. The tremendous wealth buried in Nauru's Topside, coupled with the Australian need for phosphate in the context of an imperialistic mentality, did not encourage the trustees to prepare the Nauruans for independence. Among the nations of the world, however, a sense of justice and a drive toward self-determination gained momentum. The Nauruan desire for independence and control of their land no longer could be denied.

The sixty years of mining under occupation and then trusteeship had left more than a third of the island in a state of complete destruction. Who was to restore this hollowed-out wasteland on their island? And if it could not be rehabilitated, would they be resettled on another island?

At whose expense? These questions, of vital importance to the Nauruans, were not settled when independence was granted on January 31, 1968. Rather, it took just over a quarter of a century to bring a resolution. On August 10, 1993, Nauru's suit against Australia in the International Court of Justice in the Hague was settled out of court by a "compact of settlement." Nauru would receive, over 20 years, $107 million (Australian) for restoration of the areas of Topside devastated by mining during the years of trusteeship. Though a substantial sum, in 1967 the accumulated revenue loss to the Nauruans during the trusteeship amounted to more than $300 million (Australian). Three hundred million dollars compounding at 5 percent for 26 years between 1967 and 1993 would have exceeded a billion dollars.

The Nauruans' island and their lives had been subjected to powerful external forces from the mid 1800s until independence, which transformed a self-sufficient culture into a radically different one. It was not Nauruan, nor really Western. The traditional values and patterns of life that gave meaning to the people and the culture were as eroded as the island. The wealth extracted from Topside created a market economy on Nauru that the Nauruans were obliged to join, in large part because of the devastation that World War II had brought to their island and culture. They had abandoned the island's traditional foods of fresh fish, coconut, and pandanus fruit for a diet of imported foods. Although a person could easily walk around the island in four hours, automobiles became common. Nauruans achieved independence, but a century of growing dependence on the knowledge and resources of others had not prepared them well for self-sufficiency in a world market.

While the trustees and industry officials knew the ins and outs of the phosphate industry, the Nauruans had been excluded from all aspects of the business, from the mining itself to the complexities of international markets to the management of the profits. As independence approached they had requested and been denied any assistance by those who controlled the island's wealth for almost three generations. Hammer DeRoburt, a Nauruan schoolteacher who had survived Japanese occupation as a youngster, emerged as the chief Nauruan negotiator and provided the leadership that brought independence and native control and ownership of the island's phosphate industry. As the net proceeds from the sale of phosphate accrued to their accounts, the Nauruans began to realize the tremendous wealth that had been diverted to others.

Because of the initial German control of their island, Nauruans had eventually received reparations and independence. By contrast, history treated their neighbors, the Banabans, more harshly. Each Banaban received modest royalty payments during the mining period, a one-time compensation payment of $10,000 (Australian) from the British, and relocation to another island. This difference in human political history reflected a variation in biological history. Banaba had a climate that supported few coconut trees. With no copra-trade possibilities Banaba was of little interest to the Germans in 1886. Thus, biological diversity played a major role in the human political history of these two islands, as it has in all of human history, political or otherwise.

National Geographic, in the person of Mike Holmes, again visited Nauru in 1976; the title of Holmes's article was "This Is the World's Richest Nation — All of It!" The distinctive two cultures Rosamond Rhone observed in 1921 had emulsified — the Nauruans are economic persons of a unique character. "The government offers free or low-cost everything for everybody, from owners of relatively unproductive 'coconut land' to 'phosphate land' millionaires. And nobody pays any taxes on Nauru." The sale of 2.2 million tons of phosphate rock at $60 (Australian) per ton takes care of everything. Baugie Dediya's family, the co-owners of 30 acres of phosphate land, lives in a nicely furnished, modern home with videotape TV, stereo, three washing machines, a motorboat, a motorcycle, a car, and two jeeps. Natives golf, fish for fun, and play soccer. The traditional belief "tomorrow will take care of itself" does seem to be reality.

Exactly how tomorrow will take care of itself had become a major concern for Nauru's leaders, who clearly understood that the supply of phosphate was finite. Hundreds of millions of dollars were invested — in

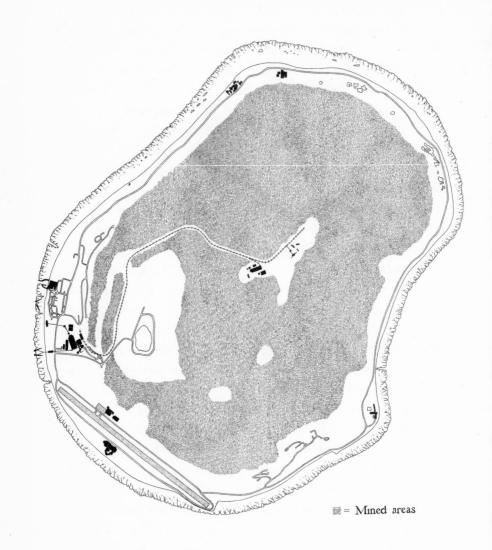

🏭 = Mined areas

Air Nauru, Nauru Pacific Shipping Line, Nauru House in Melbourne (at one time Australia's tallest building); in other office buildings and hotels in Honolulu, Washington, D.C., Houston, Guam, and the Marshall Islands; and in such diverse enterprises as a brewery in the Solomon Islands, forest land near Portland, Oregon, a phosphate fertilizer plant in India, and a musical in London — to ensure the financial well-being of future generations. By the mid 1980s the trust funds were estimated to be just over a billion dollars (Australian), but the rest of the balance sheet was a harbinger of disaster: national debt in excess of $600 million (Australian), annual revenue $60 million (Australian), and expenditures $100 million (Australian). In 1998 with the thirty-year celebration of independence and the passing of two hundred years since Western contact, the supply of unmined phosphate had dwindled — only several years to a decade of profitable mining remained. Air Nauru's five-plane fleet of jet aircraft had been reduced to one, the government payroll was not always met on time, and other signs of cash flow problems abounded.

Despite the successes or failures of financial management, in order to sustain health and a richness of life people need a worldview that gives their lives meaningful purpose. The life span for Nauruan males based upon data from 1976–1981 was under 50 years, lower than any other Pacific Island group; and a major cause is accidents — every family owns at least one vehicle despite only one paved, 18-kilometer road around the island. Nauruans are, moreover, among the most obese people on earth; their incidence of diabetes — 30 percent among those over 25 and about 50 percent in the older population — is close to if not the highest in the world. Cancer and heart disease are common, and alcoholism is a serious problem. They have acquired in full measure these and a host of other ills associated with modern civilization. Education and preventive health care are improving the situation, but the negative consequences of exchanging much of their traditional lifestyle for Western ways have been substantial.

The ecological health of Nauru is now no better than the general health of its people. Many Pacific coral islands were not biologically rich

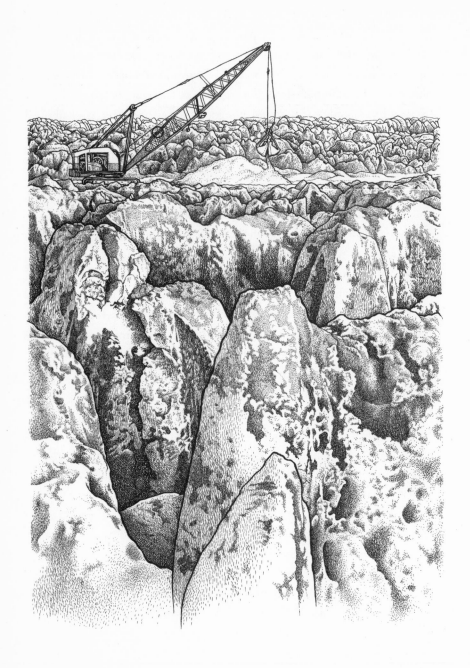

before human habitation, and Nauru was such an island. The almost total devastation of Topside coupled with the impact of about 10,000 people living on the thin coastal strip made biologically poor Nauru even poorer — most native plant species are extinct on Nauru, and 27 of the 55 species remaining are endangered or extinct. The mined-out coral pinnacles of Topside offer an inhospitable habitat for most plant life and thus most life. By natural processes it would take more than 1,000 years for Topside to undergo any significant level of biological diversity restoration.

Prior to Western influence, humans had inhabited Nauru for millennia because it supported enduring habitation, not because it was a tropical paradise. Then a new pattern of civilization came to this isolated bit of coral-created land. Within a little over a century, the Nauruans have achieved substantial monetary wealth, but this transformation has left the island and its people with immense challenges. If isolated, Nauru could no longer support its human population, nor has its people maintained the skills, knowledge, beliefs, or pattern of living necessary for enduring habitation. Why does this matter? Nauru is small, isolated, and a footnote in the history of resource exploitation, yet how big is Nauru's shadow across the earth?

Chapter Three

Nauru's Shadow

What was once a tropical paradise was changed to a jagged, uninhabitable desert of coral tombstones. Our sad history serves as a poignant example for the rest of the world of what can happen when humans disregard the good earth that sustains us.

KINZA CLODUMAR, former president of Nauru

Right after Moses had delivered the Ten Commandments, he received instructions to build an altar of unhewn stone "for if thou lift up thy tool upon it, thou hast polluted it." This scripture must mean that we are to be more mindful of the creation, more mindful of the original materials of the universe than of the artist. The altar was to stand as a reminder that we could not improve on the timeless purpose of the original material.

WES JACKSON, *Altars of Unhewn Stone*

NAURUAN CULTURE WAS SUCCESSFUL for several millennia prior to Western influence, in large measure because its cultural patterns of behavior preserved social harmony while maintaining the biological diversity required for living. Prior to the 1800s Nauruans were able to accommodate the biological, physical, and social changes they experienced on their island, yet it might not have happened that way. The earth's climate could have changed; for example, La Niña durations could have altered so that Nauru could have experienced decades, rather than years, of drought. Or the earth could have warmed, releasing the water frozen into polar ice and raising sea level many meters. In either of these situations, survival of the Nauruan people would have been problematic.

The change that totally altered the Nauruans' way of living was not climatic but social — the arrival of European civilization. The widely influential European culture — born from archaic ideas about domestication and agriculture, formalized by Greco-Roman thought, blended with Judeo-Christian religion and ethics, and enhanced by the concept of economic and scientific progress — spawned the incredibly successful, albeit destructive, societies that now dominate human existence on a planetary scale. Westerners believed, and many still believe, that they were uniquely created by God to have dominion over the earth and to employ God's other creations for their works.

Many alternative beliefs and values have been and are expressed in the West, but the central ideology and the pattern of living fits these generalizations. Consider that none of the European writings on Nauruan phosphate reject mining on the island and advocate the preservation of the traditional Nauruan way of life and the island's biological diversity. If these ideas had been mentioned, they would have been ridiculed. The human role in the world, as Westerners understood it in 1900 when phosphate was discovered on Nauru, excluded such a course of action. Even today, the advice to "leave it alone" is looked upon as radical and not regarded seriously by most government policy makers and corporate managers.

The transformations of Nauru by humans and of the Nauruan culture by Western civilization are best understood as separate but interrelated. The human transformation of Nauru did not begin with the arrival of the *Hunter* in 1798; rather, it began several thousand years earlier with the coming of the first settlers. Like many Pacific coral islands, Nauru was not biologically rich before human habitation. At the same time the soil on much of Topside was fertile by Pacific island standards; it supported hosts of plants and animals including treasured noddy birds and

important pandanus and tomano trees. The strip of land separating Topside from the ocean was among the most infertile in the Pacific islands although it was able to support abundant coconut palms.

As a general rule the number of species is a function of island size: an island that is ten times larger than another island will have twice as many species as the smaller island. Since Nauru is small, its complement of species was limited. Its remote location also constrained potential diversity because many organisms that evolved elsewhere could not get there. Thus, Nauru's biological diversity was not extensive when humans arrived. Although direct evidence is lacking, many examples of similar invasions by humans indicate that Nauru's first colonists probably modified the ecosystem and prompted species extinction.

From archaeological evidence on other Pacific islands the first human arrivals brought species from their homeland, including rats, that were new to Nauru and affected its ecosystems. Perhaps more important, humans became a dominant force in natural selection as they manipulated and employed other species to fulfill their needs and desires. From the histories of other Pacific islands we know that many organisms, such as flightless birds, became extinct after humans arrived. In time the plants, animals, and other organisms in Nauru's ecosystems responded to the new selection pressures and eventually their populations reached new equilibria.

Over the past 150 years Nauru's ecosystems have been subjected to a huge wave of alien species numbering in the thousands. Although 432 of

487 plant species living on Nauru in the 1980s were imports from else-where, we lack reports of major ecological disruptions caused by these, or other, alien species. The list of disruptions for other places in the world is long, however: prickly pear cactus and rabbits in Australia; chestnut blight, gypsy moths, tumbleweed, fire ants, starlings, zebra mussels, pur-ple loosestrife, kudzu, water chestnut, and so on in North America; and books of other examples. Nonetheless, most alien species have a hard time establishing themselves, especially in long-standing, highly evolved ecosystems. Unfortunately, when an alien does successfully establish itself, it is sometimes so successful that it may wreak havoc before selec-tion pressures establish adaptive relations.

Ecosystem equilibrium is also profoundly affected by direct human intervention. Nauru's coastal strip was severely disrupted in the distant past by cultivated coconut groves and more recently by roads, an airport, phosphate facilities, and thousands of modern houses and other build-ings. Most of the original habitat is gone, and over 50 percent of the plant diversity is imported ornamentals. The ecosystems that covered Topside on Nauru were completely devastated by phosphate mining operations that stripped surface vegetation and soil to expose the phosphate deposits surrounding the coral pinnacles. These new mining-created habitats, which now cover most of the island, are colonized by a host of plant species, but the enduring species are primarily the few remaining native plants, like ferns and tomano trees, that can tolerate such hot, soil-deficient conditions in Nauru's highly variable climate of extremely wet and dry spells. Although the mined areas that have been abandoned for decades have been colonized by some plant species, the evolution of ecosystems comparable in stability to those disrupted by mining will take thousands of years.

Most of the plant species originally on Nauru have become extinct on the island — only 8 of 17 pandanus species survive, while 27 of 55 remain-ing native species are endangered or extinct. The human-mediated impoverishment of biological diversity on Nauru is also demonstrated by comparisons of indigenous plant species on Nauru with those on other

Pacific islands of similar character. Only 58 of 142 widespread, coastal plant species found on eleven Pacific island groups are present on Nauru. Henderson Island — like Nauru except it has no recoverable phosphate and cannot support permanent human habitation — has 26 plant species not found on Nauru, while only 2 indigenous plant species on Nauru are not on Henderson. In addition, Nauru's flora harbors 17 percent weedy plant species, another indication of impoverished biological diversity and disturbed ecosystems. If the exotic species present on Nauru do not fill niches vacated by now-extinct native species, complete restoration of stable, productive ecosystems could take a very long time. Evolution is usually a slow process, especially if the raw material of evolution, genetic diversity, has become impoverished. Nine of the 17 pandanus species that supported traditional culture are extinct on Nauru, and as the rest of Topside is mined, others will become extinct. The devastation of Nauru's ecosystems has further reduced the Nauruans' scant prospects to successfully create functional ecosystems of any substantial value to humans. In the early part of the twentieth century, the Nauruans sang this prescient lament:

> By chance they discovered the heart of my home
> and gave it the name phosphate.
> If they were to ship all phosphate from my home
> there will be no place for me to go.
> Should this be the plan of the British Commission
> I shall never see my home on the hill.

The fate of Nauru's coastal strip and Topside highlights a global trend: the loss of ecosystems and the extinction of species. Although we have all witnessed countless examples of habitats and ecosystems being disrupted or destroyed for new roads, houses, marinas, shopping malls, schools, and factories, we have difficulty seeing any cumulative negative consequences resulting from these many acts. On the contrary, our cultural myths enable us to feel good about these signs of so-called progress. In biologically rich continents like the Americas it is difficult to grasp the fact that species extinction or the loss of ecosystems causes serious problems. We have lots of open space that appears inefficiently used, because we are accustomed to think of unused resources as wasted, and many of us believe that biological resources are unlimited.

The loss of biological diversity on Nauru has not prevented humans from living there, because Nauruans are no longer isolated. With their newfound wealth, they can rely on other parts of the planet for food and other needs. If the rest of the world and its biological diversity were not available to exploit, however, their situation would become untenable. The severe reduction of Topside's capacity to support diversified plant life means that 80 percent of the island's land can't provide the materials and functions of biological diversity necessary to sustain human habitation: food, shelter, medicines, local climate, recycling of nutrients, water retention, spiritual and aesthetic needs, to name a few. Below Topside on the coastal strip, the loss of habitat is of great significance because it is the most important site of the coconut palm groves, a primary source of food and vitamins. A substantial fraction of the coastal strip has been converted to roads, houses, an airport, shops, recreation facilities, and phosphate mining facilities. The condition of coconut groves and pandanus trees has deteriorated from years of abuse and neglect. In short, it would be a huge challenge for the original population of 1,000, much less the current one of 10,000, to feed and care for themselves, even with current technology; the loss of biological diversity has limited their options far more so than in the past.

Biological Diversity Loss

Scientists have established that the earth is now in the sixth mass extinction of the last 600 million years. The evidence is everywhere, yet it is not obvious over the time period of an average human life span. For example, in the 1800s the skies over the eastern United States were darkened for days by the spring migrations of billions of passenger pigeons and by enormous flocks of other birds. The passenger pigeon became extinct in

1914, and, in the last two hundred years, the absolute number of migrating American songbirds has plummeted by more than 95 percent. People now living in the eastern United States did not observe these gigantic migrations, so the occasional flock of birds migrating with the seasons, or the return of a few songbirds in the spring, seems normal. Written records show that in the past two millennia humans have been the primary cause in extinguishing more than 2,000 species of birds worldwide — which is more than 20 percent of the total extant species — and close to another 2,000 are endangered.

Forty million bison inhabited the Great Plains of North America in 1798 at the same time that the *Hunter* encountered Nauru; but in less than a century the population of plains bison was only several hundred. When Europeans began their explorations into the Pacific, the great whales were so abundant that they were seen in the hundreds by anyone who put to sea. Ecotourists now spend days seeking a glimpse of the few that remain. Four or five decades ago motorists in the United States scraped layers of insects from their car grills; now a Sunday drive in many places of the United States yields but a few stains.

This devastation of the earth's biota has been carefully documented in thousands of studies, which, in turn, have been summarized and analyzed in hundreds of books. It is not a question of whether or not we will have a mass extinction, but of how severe it will be. We focus on birds and large mammals because we identify with such creatures and have empathy for them. Their extinctions are the tip of the iceberg, though — mere indicators of what is happening to the health of ecosystems. If the population of a major herbivore or a top carnivore in an ecosystem has substantially diminished, or become extinct, the whole ecosystem may be in trouble, especially if the cause is linked to organisms lower on the food chain.

Humans have been transforming the planet for tens of thousands of years; the effects are now everywhere visible from hundreds of miles in space. Within the past several centuries the ever-accelerating scale of transformation has made extinctions global, and the extinctions have penetrated deeply throughout the fabric of life.

The exact number of species that inhabit the earth is unknown, but the 1.7 million named species probably represent between 1 and 25 percent of the total. If we do not know what exists, though, we cannot know what is missing. Even so, it appears that we are losing between a thousand and several tens of thousands of species each year. Overall, the prehuman extinction rate was roughly one to several species per year. The tragedy of the tropical rain forests exemplifies the planetary crisis of species extinction. In the past one hundred years humans have cut down about half of the world's tropical rain forests. Extinction has eliminated between 1 and 10 percent of the species that lived there. Nobody knows the exact number, but we have lost many species in the blink of an eye, on an evolutionary timescale. Life forms created over millions of years of evolution have disappeared forever. If humans cut down all but 1 percent of the original rain forests over the next one hundred years, as is anticipated by some, we will lose between 50 and 75 percent of the rain forest species.

Although the Nauruans have not yet faced the full consequences of the loss of the contribution of their island's biological diversity to their well being, they will soon have exhausted its phosphate, their primary source of financial wealth. Although it was clear from the day phosphate was discovered that it would be used up, phosphate was never directly connected to human survival on Nauru. Water, in contrast, is another matter. In the distant past Nauru's freshwater supply from wells, ponds, and rain was limited during droughts; now, it is always insufficient because of the almost tenfold increase in population. A desalination plant now meets this need, but until the early 1990s water was imported on the same transport ships that hauled away phosphate. While the depletion of phosphate is forcing economic changes, the mining and depletion of Nauru's freshwater aquifer will make the island far less habitable.

Overpopulation

Earth, like Nauru, is finite, an island in the ocean of space. Understanding this is easy: we have all seen pictures of Earth taken from the moon that depict the stark finiteness of our planet. Humans everywhere are confronted daily with more evidence that we are pushing the limits of the planet's support capacities, yet we behave as though we have no knowledge of these limitations. The approach to resources — energy, mineral, or biological — has been to consider them infinite, sustainable, or substitutable. This would be a reasonable position if the scale of human activity were small compared to the available resources, but it becomes problematic when the human use of a resource is projected to exhaust the resource. The lens of Nauru focuses the challenge. With their phosphate-derived wealth, the Nauruans will — so long as their investments last — be able to buy from the rest of the world any items necessary to make up for shortages. But after the money runs out, they will have few choices: emigrate or radically restructure their scale and pattern of living. One way or another, modern humanity must resolve its resource challenges here; emigration to another planet is not an option.

Trade with the rest of the world has not only enabled the Nauruans to survive quite well on a biologically and materially impoverished island, but it has also allowed an ecologically unsustainable population size. The expenditure of energy coupled with creative technologies and trade has permitted the movement of phosphate to the rest of the world and the transport to Nauru of the materials needed to sustain 10,000 people. The biological resources of the island provide for only a minuscule fraction of the needs of this population. If disconnected from the rest of the world, the population would dwindle.

While it is quite clear that the current population of Nauru is larger than the number of people who can live there self-sufficiently, the number of people who can live sustainably on the planet is an open question. The rate of growth of the population accelerated for a long time. For example, it took about 180 years to double from half a billion (1650) to 1 billion (1830), while to go from 2 billion (1930) to 4 billion (1975) took only 45 years. Although the future is uncertain, the growth rate is no longer accelerating; that is, the time it takes for the human population to double is lengthening. If this trend continues, the population will eventually stop growing. While this is good news in the long term, over 80 million additional humans are still being added to the population each year, and similar increases are projected for many years.

Although most people accept that there is a limit to the human population the earth can support, that limit cannot be precisely determined. Why? Because the variables are so many and, to make matters worse, because unknown variables always lurk in the background. When Antoni van Leeuwenhoek predicted in 1679 that maximum human population was about 13 billion, he did not know that human activities were causing a mass biological diversity extinction, that cutting down tropical forests could change local and global climates, or that tractors would allow one person to till hundreds of acres. Despite these many variables, scientists and others have made numerous predictions; 65 factually based calculations have a low median of 8 billion people and a high median of 16 billion, with a mean of about 12 billion. These values are of immediate concern because many demographers have calculated that the population will plateau around 12 billion sometime in the second half of the twenty-first century.

However, none of these calculations takes sustainability into account; that is, the calculations are essentially for a population size at a certain time, not for one that could be maintained for thousands of years. If we cannot do the calculation precisely for a point in time, we have no hope of performing a dynamic calculation that would be valid for hundreds or thousands of years. Both types of calculations are worthwhile, however, because the results give us a sense of reality — the threshold of monumental disaster. The maximum population size numbers tell us that as the world population reaches 6 billion, we are approaching disaster because a population this size is likely to be sustained for only a few generations.

The number of organisms in an ecosystem is the result of interaction between the species' biological growth potential and the environmental resistance that prevents all organisms from realizing their potential. Under ideal conditions, for instance, one bacterium could increase to 2.2

$\times$ 10^{43} bacteria in 48 hours with a mass roughly a thousand times that of the earth. Environmental resistance — climate, abiotic resources like water and nutrients, toxic waste buildup, and biological factors like parasites, predators, and competition for resources — prevent every population of organisms from realizing its growth potential.

An animal species may have several long-term stable population sizes, each depending on unique environmental resistance factors. And each of these stable populations, or carrying capacities, represents the number of individuals of a species that the ecosystem can support under the specified conditions. If the environmental resistance factors do not change, the ecosystem does not change and the population size remains stable. Things never stay the same, of course. Over time major factors in the environmental resistance will vary and the population size will change.

The carrying capacity concept has predictive value in managing wildlife and in determining the sizes of populations in natural ecosystems. You might ask, if carrying capacity applies to pheasants, deer, and grizzly bears, why doesn't it apply to humans? It does. Like all organisms, humans are subject to the laws of ecology, but we can't calculate the carrying capacity for humans with any precision because we can manipulate our ecosystems in profound ways. We have become extremely adept at tapping stored-up natural resources, especially energy, water, and soil fertility; and in doing so we establish what appears to be a higher carrying capacity. With the domestication of animals and plants and the emergence of agriculture 10,000 years ago, stored-up resources were used first within local ecosystems. Over the last two centuries, however, the earth's resource stockpiles have been used globally. This worldwide exchange of resources, as well as exceedingly clever technologies, has increased a region's carrying capacity by overcoming local constraints.

Life on Earth is possible because energy flows from the sun; despite exceptions, essentially all the energy that runs Earth's biotic enterprise is captured in photosynthesis by plants, algae, and cyanobacteria. We have been able to increase population by co-opting about 40 percent of the net land photosynthesis and a smaller fraction from aquatic environments;

by contrast, 10,000 years ago the estimated world population of 4 million humans used less than 0.005 percent of net land photosynthesis. Consider again, for example, the Great Plains of North America where, prior to European habitation, 40 million bison and thousands of humans and smaller animals lived off the energy supplied by the grasses and other plants. We now farm and ranch that land, and in doing so we probably support an even larger biomass of animals — primarily chickens, pigs, and cows, as well as millions of humans — by employing industrial agriculture.

It may sound good that we have improved the ecosystem's productivity by relying on industrial agriculture. Closer analysis, though, indicates that this may be a short-term phenomenon. When microorganisms, invertebrates, grasses, bison, deer, antelope, and native Americans were the prime players in the ecosystem, the whole system ran on sunshine and was biologically more stable. The ecological "books" were in balance, and some items like topsoil usually were improving.

Industrial agriculture has increased the apparent carrying capacity by using vast amounts of fossil fuels to make fertilizers, insecticides, and herbicides in addition to the fuels used to raise seeds and to run the machinery that works the soil and disperses seeds and chemicals. For each calorie of food produced, close to 3 calories of fossil fuel energy are consumed on the farm — energy that did not come from this year's sunshine. In addition, water is pumped from the ground for irrigation; some of this water comes from aquifers that are drained faster than they are filled. These farming methods have led to a massive loss of topsoil through water, wind, and splash erosion. Over the past 150 years Iowa has lost 50 percent of its fertile topsoil to erosion, while the current rate of loss is 30 tons per hectare per year compared to a formation rate of 1 ton per hectare per year. In contrast, undisturbed grasslands and forests have erosion rates of .02 and .07 tons per hectare per year, respectively. In the long run this kind of agriculture reduces the carrying capacity of ecosystems, as it has done already in many areas around the world, primarily in ecosystems less resilient than parts of the Great Plains. The apparent success of current industrial agriculture has led many people to believe that the earth's long-term human carrying capacity is far greater than it really is.

Biologists also have indirect evidence that puts the size of our current population in an ecological category of its own. How many individuals exist in a population within a certain area depends on the organism's size. Bacteria are small and billions of many species exist in 1 cubic meter of forest soil. Field mice are much larger than bacteria and only thousands exist in 1 square kilometer of grassland. Deer are about the size of humans, and 4 deer per square kilometer is a normal distribution in a forest-meadow habitat. Primates like howler monkeys and mountain gorillas are rare, and their density of habitation is a fraction of an individual for many square kilometers. A human is a large primate weighing about 50 kilograms, so we would predict human densities similar to those of primates or at least similar to those of other large animals like deer, wolves, or bears. When we compare the current human population with that of 50-kilogram or larger nondomesticated land vertebrates, however, the global human population density is now 100 times greater than that of any other similar-sized animal, past or present. Our global population size is an ecological aberration. The reason is simply explained: First, directly or indirectly, humans use huge amounts of the energy acquired by plants, at the expense of other species. Second, intelligence and communication have enabled huge human populations to exist almost everywhere on the planet by cleverly employing technologies to increase present-day carrying capacities.

Not only is the human population enormous, but our local densities are gigantic, too. In cities like New York City or Hong Kong humans have densities of tens of thousands per square kilometer. In an entire country like Holland, an average of 440 people live in each square kilometer — a phenomenal density when compared with other large animals. The current Dutch population could not maintain its lifestyle, or most likely any lifestyle, if it was limited to subsisting on resources from Holland alone. The Dutch would need at least fifteen times more area to obtain the resources they currently use. Such densities are possible in cities and most countries because people are taking resources from elsewhere.

In 1798, Thomas Malthus, a British political economist, warned Western industrial society that human population growth would be halted by natural causes unless we controlled our numbers. Humans have failed, however, to establish a stable population because beliefs and economic incentives support contrary behavior and because our technologies enable us to overcome local limits in the present. The export of Western culture and economies eliminated constraints on population growth in many places around the planet. The result? A world population that has doubled in just over forty years.

Over the past hundred years, though, the patterns of change experienced by populations around the globe have exhibited enormous variability. In the early twentieth century, the populations in western European countries were growing rapidly, but by the early 1980s some had completed a demographic transition to zero population growth. Over a one-hundred-year period birth rates had dropped to equal death rates because of availability of contraceptive technologies, widespread education, lower child mortality, higher living standards, and the depletion of places to export excess population.

For most of the twentieth century nonindustrialized countries have witnessed tremendous jumps in their populations, but in the last several decades fertility rates in many have fallen even faster than were experienced during the demographic transition in European countries. This is not because living standards have risen; contraceptives, greater education and economic opportunities primarily for women, and media information on population and family planning have paved the way. Other situations, like economic and social deterioration in the former Soviet Union, have resulted in dramatic fertility declines. Although trends can be identified, the world is composed of myriad cultures, with each expressing a dynamic pattern of population change.

Climate Change

Prior to European influence, Nauru's population size appeared to result from an interactive cultural response to climate — primarily the frequent La Niña–associated droughts. Perhaps because of Nauru's small size and the frequency of drought, Nauruan culture adapted quickly to the island's biological and physical realities. Culturally created patterns of living stabilized their population and preserved enough of the island's biological diversity to meet their needs. Today, however, Nauruans are threatened by more than La Niña–associated droughts as global industrialization and deforestation change the earth's atmosphere, which of course influences the global climate.

The earth's climate derives from greenhouse gases like carbon dioxide and water in our atmosphere that allow light energy to pass through but that absorb some of the longer wavelengths of heat energy radiating from the planet. As a consequence, its climate is controlled by the amount of sunlight, and subsequently heat energy, that reaches the atmosphere, the land, and the oceans. Latitude dictates the amount of energy received; equatorial regions get more heat than do polar regions. The dynamic nature of global climate mainly results from physical processes, like ocean currents and winds, that equalize this difference. Certainly these processes are major causes of local weather. The solar energy input to the earth also depends on the variable output from the sun and the earth's changing distance to it. Local energy input is related to surface cover (water, snow, ice, brown soil, green plants) and local atmospheric composition (clouds, water vapor, particulate matter, sulfates). The equation is, in a word, complex, as is evident in our poor record for weather prediction. Even though we spend billions of dollars and employ thousands of people to collect and analyze atmospheric data to predict weather for the next several days, we know from personal experience that near-term weather forecasts are only modestly accurate. It is not surprising that we can't predict in any detail next year's, much less next century's, weather.

Even so, human activities have influenced local climates for millennia.

Within the past hundred years we now know our activities influence global climate. Climate change has figured prominently in all of human history. What is different now, though, is that human activities on a global scale — deforestation and burning of fossil fuels, to name a couple — are big contributors to the rise in atmospheric concentrations of carbon dioxide of about 30 percent over the last hundred years, from 280 parts per million to over 360 parts per million. Carbon dioxide absorbs radiant energy at some wavelengths not absorbed by other greenhouse gases; thus, when the carbon dioxide concentration in the atmosphere increases to a new level, more heat energy is retained and the planet becomes warmer until a new equilibrium is reached. If no carbon dioxide were in the atmosphere, the planet's temperature would drop below the freezing point of water, and life as we know it would not have evolved. By contrast, if we had as much carbon dioxide as Venus's sizzling-hot atmosphere, Earth too would be several hundred degrees Celsius. Again, the conditions would not permit life.

Atmospheric scientists around the world have reached consensus that this human-caused rise in atmospheric carbon dioxide and other greenhouse gases will warm the planet considerably during the next several hundred years, depending on how high the levels of carbon dioxide and other greenhouse gases go. But nobody knows how much or how long it will take. The greater energy differential between equatorial and polar regions may increase the number and severity of storms. Local climate changes, which determine the regions that will be wetter or drier, are difficult if not impossible to predict.

Global warming would not be good for the people of Nauru. If the South Pole warms enough to release say 10 percent of the water now stored in snow and ice, the coastal strip of land on Nauru would be submerged and the island would be uninhabitable. Worldwide, the more than a billion people who live close to sea level might lose their homes. Where will they live and how will they obtain the necessities of life if their homes and associated biological support systems are under water?

Climate change will necessitate the migration of organisms and whole ecosystems to areas where prospects for survival are better — a move that will lead to the extinction of others. Many will be unable to make the move because of the formidable barriers imposed by humans — highways, agricultural land, cities, and industrial areas. The more quickly the climate changes, the more difficult migration will be; and the rate of extinction will accelerate accordingly. Humans will experience severe turmoil caused by the immense challenges associated with adjusting to warmer and more unstable climates. The loss of biological diversity will make the adjustments even more problematic.

This episode of civilization-disrupting global warming caused by greenhouse gases may, ironically, trigger a devastating global cooling, perhaps another ice age. Chicago at 42°N latitude is blustery cold in February, while London and Paris at 49°N latitude only have temperatures below freezing occasionally. The climates of North America and Europe are vastly different because of the Gulf Stream. These currents are part of a complex and incompletely understood global pattern of ocean circulation that mixes ocean waters and helps to redistribute equatorial solar energy. Paleoclimatologists have established that the ocean currents are not constant; they flip from time to time to different patterns. We now have evidence that when the Gulf Stream no longer reaches into the North Sea—a phenomenon that apparently occurred during recent ice ages and during the cold period beginning about 12,700 years ago—Europe's climate becomes like North America's and the rest of the world gets colder.

The Gulf Stream sinks in the North Sea and off the southern coast of Greenland because when dry winds blow across it, large quantities of water evaporate, and its salt content rises and eventually it becomes denser than the water below. To balance the volume of water moving north in the surface Gulf Stream, the sunken dense water flows south. However, if the Gulf Stream is diluted, the water might not sink, which could flip ocean currents to another pattern. This could happen if increased greenhouse gases either prompt more rainfall in the higher latitudes or make Greenland's ice melt. Either event could cause excess freshwater to flow into the Gulf Stream, preventing it from becoming denser than the water below and from sinking.

Without the warming effect of the Gulf Stream, it is easy to understand why Europe would quickly get cold like North America. But why would the entire planet get colder? Although the reasons are uncertain, one model indicates that rearranging the ocean's circulation could lead to less evaporation in the tropics. Since water vapor is an important greenhouse gas, this decrease could cool the planet. Regardless of the mechanism, previous cold periods in Europe not only have been correlated with ocean current flips but also with global cooling. These facts and the possible connection between global warming and global cooling should be sobering for a world intoxicated with fossil fuels and intent on cutting down forests.

Climate and human habitation are intimately connected everywhere. Releasing the vast quantities of carbon sequestered in fossil fuels will change the climate throughout the planet, and the resulting changes will affect global patterns of human habitation. Although history tells us that changes to the earth's climate are inevitable, forcing climate change by burning millions of years of stored sunshine in a few hundred years will probably hurt our long-term interests.

Although Nauru is remote and little known to much of the world, its story has great meaning for all of us. Nauru's history clearly reveals the myriad and interconnected environmental challenges humans face, including biodiversity loss, population size, and climate change — all extraordinarily important and demanding our attention. In order to understand the current dilemmas posed by these challenges and to begin to address them, we must more fully explore cultural patterns, both those that have achieved sustainability and those that have failed to do so.

Chapter Four

Living the Myths

History teaches us nothing, but only punishes [us] for not learning its lessons.

VLADIMIR KLIUCHESKY, quoted in Robert Heilbroner,
Twenty-First Century Capitalism

[Indigenous peoples'] very survival has depended upon their ecological awareness and adaptation. . . . These communities are the repositories of vast accumulations of traditional knowledge and experience that link humanity with its ancient origins. Their disappearance is a loss for the larger society, which could learn a great deal from their traditional skills in sustainably managing very complex ecological systems. It is a terrible irony that as formal development reaches more deeply into rain forest, deserts, and other isolated environments, it tends to destroy the only cultures that have proved able to thrive in these environments.

BRUNDTLAND REPORT

OUR ANCESTORS EVOLVED in Africa, where 5 million years ago they separated from the lineage we share with chimpanzees. The earliest representatives of the family *Hominidae* appeared perhaps 4 million years ago and the earliest members of the genus *Homo* between 2 to 3 million years ago. *Homo erectus,* the first of our line to migrate out of Africa, evolved in another million years. Emigration probably continued to take place, and perhaps migration back into Africa from elsewhere occurred, too, but paleoanthropologists now believe that, from 100,000 to 200,000 years ago, the modern form of *Homo sapiens* evolved in Africa and began to spread throughout the world, perhaps replacing human populations representing earlier out-migrations. The selective advantage of these modern humans probably depended on their high level of intelligence, which allowed for complex communication and thus their greater capacity for culture. As modern humans populated the earth, they adapted culturally to a wide variety of environments. Traditional Nauruan culture is simply one of innumerable ways of living that humans have created over the past several million years.

Culture creation and biological evolution are different, yet they are grounded in the same processes — interactions between an individual's genetic constitution and the physical, biological, and social environment. To understand human cultural possibilities, we consider first the relations among genes, environment, biological evolution, and cultural change.

The genes of an organism represent its genotype; and the expression of these genes, as influenced by the environment, creates its phenotype. The human phenotype comprises all of the physical and functional characteristics of an individual, such as five fingers on each hand, eye color, height, the ability to see red but not ultraviolet light, speech, mathematical or athletic ability, and the manifestations of biochemical, physiological, and morphological conditions that enable two or more individuals to relate to each other for purposes of mating, fighting, cooperating, or playing. Our genes have not evolved for the purpose of producing a specific phenotype; rather, the phenotype manifests a particular adaptation to an environment, which allows the individual to survive and produce offspring. Specific abilities, like playing soccer, are not connected with survival or reproduction, but running, passing a ball in anticipation of where the receiver will be, or avoiding collisions with other players do represent traits related to survival.

Physical and behavioral traits that give survival advantage to an individual, or to a group whose members share the genes underlying the adaptive traits, are preserved over generations because they are adaptive in the experienced environment. Social animals have evolved because the social traits provide the group with a reproductive advantage over those groups, or individuals, without these traits. In some animals, like ants and termites, much of the social behavior is not learned but instinctive. In such organisms all individuals of a given caste behave in the same way under a given set of conditions. In other social animals, like dogs, instinctive behaviors are present, but the behavior patterns of a dog combine instinctive and learned behaviors. All of the dog's behaviors, however, have a genetic basis; that is, the ability to learn and the predisposition to learn some things more quickly than others are coded in the genes.

The ability of social animals such as wolves, humans, and elephants to organize into groups and interact with each other and their environment in collective or individual ways has a genetic basis, just as having five fingers on a human hand does. Although most people have five fingers, an individual may have a different number of digits depending on certain combinations of genes. In addition, the number of digits may diverge from five as a result of environmental factors present during the development of a fetus's hand. In an oversimplified and artificial dichotomy, the genetic component can be considered "nature" and the environmental component "nurture." Most people have little difficulty talking about what is nature and what is nurture with respect to the number of digits on a hand. People do, however, have considerable difficulty in evaluating the nature-nurture components of qualities like human intelligence or of human behavior because physical bases for these traits are deeply hidden in our brain and genes, and are not obvious like the number of fingers. In addition, nurture and nature are extremely difficult to separate in such character traits that combine instinct and learning.

The now-famous Minnesota Twins Study, in which identical and fraternal twins raised together or apart were analyzed, has provided data on how much human behavior and intelligence are influenced by nature. Although the details of this work and related studies are controversial for reasons indicated above, their authors conclude that a person's genes underlie much of that person's behavior and intelligence — but certainly not all. Thus, identical twins are genetically the same, but each twin has a measure of unique capacities and personality traits, because each has been raised in a unique environment. Genes specify potential, and the environment establishes the specific phenotype within a range of possible phenotypes. Consider, for example, performance in mathematics or art. In any first-grade class a teacher observes a wide range of student performance in either area. When a teacher expends more time, effort, and materials, each student's performance improves, but differences remain. The twins study has established that diversity arises because of differences in both nature and nurture, in addition to the interactions between these two broad determinants of biological expression.

The creation of cultures is in some respects similar to the formation of species. If two groups of people from one culture enter two new places, in time two new cultures will emerge. Each group will make choices about how to relate to the new environment and to each other, and will learn and establish new ways of doing things that are different from the original culture. These patterns of living will be taught to new generations. Like our two hypothetical cultures, all cultures result from the cumulative interactions between a group of humans and where they have lived. Because of the tremendous variations possible in human phenotypes, in environments, and in available choices, patterns of living vary widely among cultures. Indeed, cultural diversity, like all biological phenomena, is constrained only by the laws of nature and genetic endowment.

Nauruan culture illustrates one pattern of living by which its people in adapting to their environment created an enduring mode of habitation. For several thousand years prior to European influence, Nauru's ecological books balanced, and the island's life-support systems were maintained for its inhabitants. Throughout the last century the European, market-based pattern of living that overwhelmed the traditional

Nauruan culture has relentlessly reduced Nauru's capacity to support human habitation. Hundreds of other cultural groups also elucidate our current dilemma: the current global market economy lacks the long-term capacity to provide for human well-being and to preserve life-support systems. We consider five such groups in this chapter: two hunter-gatherer cultures and three nonindustrial agricultural cultures. Their successes and failures in achieving enduring habitation provide insights into the predicament confronting all of us.

Archeological and paleobiological analyses of artifacts and fossils indicate that humans similar to ourselves walked upright on the African savannas several million years ago. Beginning only about 10,000 years ago, in locations around the globe humans became agriculturists and within several thousand years formed the prehistoric hierarchical societies from which most contemporary societies are derived. Thus for more than 99 percent of our history humans were closely associated with their local ecosystems as gatherers and hunters. Humans lived in small bands of 20 to 50 individuals, and their cultures were as diverse as the lands that sustained them. Although most of these cultures have been obliterated, leaving scant records, a few still survive in some of the harshest environments on earth. Let's consider two groups of hunter-gatherers: the Australian aborigines, whose ancestors reached that continent about 60,000 years ago, and the Kalahari !Kung, who arrived in southern Africa millennia ago.

Australian Aborigines

Beginning about two and a half million years ago, the earth entered a cyclical climate pattern that produced episodes of glaciation when northern parts of Asia, Europe, and North America were buried under thousands of feet of ice. With frozen water piled high on the land, the sea level dropped and exposed hundreds of kilometers of continental shelf. During one of these glacial periods, 40,000 to 100,000 years ago, New Guinea was almost continuous with the Asian mainland, and humans ventured into Australia for the first time. Stretching from New Guinea to Java to Borneo to Australia, a chain of islands existed with each island in sight of, or just over the horizon from, the next island. In simple boats, the ancestors of the Australian aborigines island-hopped until they came upon the northern shore of an immense continent. Over thousands of years they moved throughout Australia among a multitude of habitats ranging from tropical rain forests to mountain forests to grasslands to parched deserts. These habitats and the original culture of these ancestors molded each other, spawning hundreds of variant cultures. More than five hundred languages and dialects emerged. When the first European eyes fell on the southern continent in the sixteenth or seventeenth century, the aborigine population was about a half million. A few places in Australia might be considered tropical paradises, despite their exceptionally large number of poisonous snakes. Most of the continent, however, is harsh and inhospitable to twentieth-century humans. This is reflected in the fact that fewer than twenty million people, supported by modern technologies, live there on a landmass equivalent in size to that of the continental United States. It was into these austere ecosystems that the ancestral aborigines ventured and thrived.

Precise knowledge about the diversity of Australian cultures has been lost because the English who colonized Australia as a continental jail had little interest in the ethnology of aborigines. Aborigines were low on European culture's Ladder of Nature. Some English colonials claimed that the aborigines were not even human, deeming it appropriate to remove them from the land so it could be put to better use. The Tasmanian aborigines, who were marooned when the seas rose at the end of the last ice age, were hunted almost to extinction by the English. Mainland aborigines fared a little better, and more of their cultures survived.

Although the aborigines had intricate social interactions, they had no governments, no chiefs, no concept of war, no military, no organized religions, no agriculture, no domesticated plants or animals except the half-tamed dingo, no private ownership of land, no concept of material wealth, few personal possessions, and no interest in acquiring more. In 1770, when Captain Cook's men gave them cloth and trinkets, they left these gifts on the beach or in the woods as they walked away. At the time, their behavior was unlike that of any peoples with whom Western explorers had come in contact.

Aborigine cosmology is embodied in the Dreaming, a translated term that describes a way of thought. The Dreamtime is the time of world-creation, of ancestral heroes, and great events, yet — paradoxically, to a Western way of thinking — native Australians do not conceive of it as time past, in a linear Western sense. Indeed, past, present, and future are not clearly distinguished and are viewed as contemporaneous, not because the aborigines are unable to conceptualize time in that way, but because they do it differently. Just as a Jew or Christian might say that God is everywhere, an aborigine might say the Dreaming is "every-when." Dreaming paths, created with the spirit world, established the society. Traditional aboriginal society was thus an expression of the Dreaming that had effected the deep connections between people and place. The source of life for any individual came from the place where the spirit child entered a woman and animated a fetus. A child's totemic affiliation reflected a spiritual lineage that was different from his or her blood lineage.

Each family was associated with a band of usually fewer than fifty persons, which functioned as the hunting and foraging unit. Food was shared among all members of the band regardless of each member's contribution. Within the band and among other bands that occupied the same area, groupings other than family existed and were based on distant lineage, totemic association, specific sites, and relations to the land. The members of the band did not own the land on which they lived and over which they traveled; rather, they were so deeply connected to the spirits of their physical place that people and land were one. All of these relations made each person aware of his or her place within the society and established within a group the pattern of interactions among its members.

The Australian aborigines had few possessions, their technologies were simple, and their needs were easily met. In many places the climate was mild and they chose not to wear clothes. Division of labor was based on gender, and at times children assisted adults and learned skills from their elders. As the primary gatherer, a woman's equipment was a digging stick and a dilly bag, while as the hunter, a man's tools were a spear and a spear thrower. Men could also gather, since during childhood, they learned which plants were edible, and women also hunted. Most bands made no permanent structures and moved about the land, looking for plants and following animals. With so few material possessions and with nature's bounty easily accessible, even in times of drought, the aborigines filled their time by making art and music, dancing, and storytelling. These acts ritualistically connected everything and united people and land in a spiritual whole.

The Dreaming bonded each group of bands to a place; and since aborigines maintained no surplus to fight over, expansion and territorial conflicts were limited. Although disputes were apparently rare, sometimes they did arise over personal relations or over the casting of spells that were believed to cause a person, or group, misfortune.

Aboriginal myths connected past, present, and future. Life existed; therefore, it was natural. In contrast, death was not existence and hence was unnatural. People had to learn how to die, and some aborigines appeared to have the capacity to elect the time of their death. They had no concept of sin nor of life after death, although the spirit that animated a fetus, and was part of a person's being, did not die with the person.

Kalahari !Kung

The !Kung are an African people of small stature with light brown skin. They live in what is now the northwest corner of Botswana and in parts of neighboring Namibia and Angola, areas so harsh and unproductive that herders and agriculturalists avoided them until the second half of the twentieth century when population pressures pushed such people into these marginal lands. The exclamation point in !Kung is pronounced as a click and is characteristic of Khoisan languages. They lived as hunter-gatherers during most of the twentieth century, although they were probably in contact with agriculturists and herders for hundreds or perhaps thousands of years. Even in the 1960s the !Kung appeared minimally influenced by the outside world, although they used metal weapons and implements. Anthropologists who studied the !Kung in the middle of the twentieth century have given us an extensive and thorough picture of how these hunter-gatherers lived until recently.

Although the well-studied Nyae Nyae !Kung and the Dobe !Kung represent different !Kung cultures, we consider !Kung culture as a whole, because we want to show in broad terms how the !Kung related to each other and their environment. Contrary to Hobbes's statement that originally human existence was "nasty, brutish, and short," among the !Kung food was plentiful, violent conflicts were rare, and about 10 percent of the people were over 60 years old, a percentage reached by most agricultural or industrial communities only in the twentieth century.

The !Kung were immediate-return hunter-gatherers in that they did not store food nor did they have complicated capital in the form of permanent shelters or elaborate tools. They had a vast knowledge of the plants and animals in their habitat, and they could draw on a diversity of food sources in all seasons. At any time a band might have two or three days' supply of food on hand. One group of Dobe !Kung had 85 edible plant species and 223 animal species from which to choose. Ninety percent of the plants in their diet came from 23 species, and only 17 species of the animals available to them were hunted regularly. The major item in their diet was mongongo nuts, an excellent food. A 210-gram portion contains just over 1,200 calories and 56 grams of protein, which is equivalent to 5.5 kilograms of cooked rice and 392 grams of lean beef. The mongongo forests were within easy walking distance of many water-holes — less than 10 kilometers — and only in the dry season was longer travel sometimes required. When a !Kung was asked why he didn't plant crops, he replied: "Why should I plant when there are so many mongongo nuts in the world?" The average daily Dobe !Kung diet contained about 2,100 calories with 93 grams of protein as compared to a calculated requirement of about 2,000 calories and 60 grams of protein for their body size and level of activity. In addition, it is clear from historical accounts that food was readily available and sufficient for !Kung needs.

The !Kung spent most of their time socializing and dancing, and their conversation often focused on food and hunting. How much time did it take to acquire and prepare food? Since making tools, playing, hunting, food gathering, performing rituals, and spending time with one's family were not always distinct activities, anthropologists had difficulty judging how much time the !Kung and other hunter-gatherers spent on food-related activities. The calculation was further complicated because food sometimes was easy to get, while at other times, as in the dry season, it took more time. However, anthropologists calculated that the amount of time an adult spent on all food-related activities varied from 2 to 8 hours per day with an average of 4 to 6 hours. The acquisition of food took a fraction of this time. To make a valid comparison with the time spent by industrialized people, one would have to sum the time spent not only shopping and preparing food but also earning the money to buy the kitchen, the food, and the appliances to prepare it, as well as the energy, services, and materials — gasoline, car, roads, food storage, police, and so on — associated with these food-related activities.

Sharing meat was an important stabilizing ritual in !Kung society. Plants and small animals were shared within the family, as well as with close relatives and friends, but large animals like elands, springboks, warthogs, or wildebeests were shared by everybody in the camp. The !Kung hunted in groups of two to five men, and hunting parties were informally organized with men deciding, or being asked, to join. When an animal was killed, it belonged to, and was distributed by, the owner of the arrow that first penetrated the animal deep enough to deliver the poison that killed it. Ownership of an arrow was established in one of three ways: a hunter might make an arrow, he might be given one, or he might be loaned one. If the arrow that killed the animal had been loaned to the hunter, the animal belonged to the arrow's owner, not to the hunter.

The freshly butchered parts of an animal were first given by the owner of the arrow to the hunters, who in turn divided their portions and gave them to others, usually family and friends. These people then gave portions to others and so on until essentially everybody had a portion. In one instance, 63 acts of giving were observed in a group of bands comprising about 100 individuals, and some giving was probably missed. Men who may have never killed a large animal or who may never have hunted still received meat. Although sometimes this free-riding was a problem, the sharing of meat served to bind the group together.

Since access to food sources and waterholes came with membership in a band, a !Kung did not function as an individual but rather as a member of a band. At the same time, bands were flexible groups that were constantly changing. Any one person or family had rights in several bands as a function of inherited or marital relations. This social flexibility avoided potential problems by simply allowing a person to move to another band.

The !Kung of the mid twentieth century had few possessions. A digging stick, leather bags, scraping and cutting implements, water containers, cooking utensils, a bow and arrows, and a quiver were the tools for acquiring and making necessities. Musical instruments, children's toys, jewelry, and beads were common possessions also. Together, these items would weigh about 60 kilograms and fit in two leather sacks. !Kung of earlier times certainly had fewer possessions, and everything they owned could be made from readily available materials.

The !Kung were always exchanging gifts. Their pattern of gift giving was an important ritual for bringing people together into friendly relations and reducing ill will and jealousy. Gifts were not exotic treasures but everyday objects like arrows, pipes, ostrich-eggshell-bead necklaces, thumb pianos, or digging sticks. By giving a gift, the giver and receiver became bonded. By accepting a gift, the receiver assumed an obligation to return a gift of equivalent value sometime in the future — a few weeks to several years. If a gift was owed, a person might ask for an item, and it would usually be given. With everybody giving a gift to somebody else, friendly relations were promoted and goods were constantly circulating. The giving ritual was also a social check against the accumulation of objects because no one possessed an item for any length of time. It made little sense to accumulate things since most items could be readily made. Besides, having a lot to move to the next camp made little sense.

Although these characterizations of the Australian aborigines and !Kung may not apply to all of the hunter-gatherer cultures that have existed over the millennia, they offer valuable insights about what traits among humans are innate or universal, or both, and those that are dependent upon cultural circumstances. Clearly, humans can establish sustainable relations with their natural surroundings even in austere ecosystems. In the global economic culture many characteristics assumed to be either human nature or fundamental to all human societies are actually culture dependent.

The assumptions about universal human nature underlying our market economy are questionable. First, since neither aborigines nor !Kung accumulated many material goods, we suggest that the emphasis by our market society on acquisition of such goods is a socially conditioned behavior and is not innate. Likewise, nonacquisitiveness appears to be a culturally learned behavior. Humans certainly have the capacity for both types of behavior. Second, as evident from the !Kung apportionment of the hunt, it is not human nature to link production with distribution. In addition to sharing resources, the ritual of giving among the !Kung indicates that selfishness is not a universally expressed trait. Both aborigines and !Kung had sufficient, if not excess, resources for their needs. This situation supports the thesis that the current economic notion of scarcity is a social construct, not a condition of human existence. In these hunter-gatherer societies, life's different activities formed a continuum, and the separation of work from other aspects of living was not necessary to economic production. Finally, the !Kung and the aborigines lived in egalitarian societies. They lacked social classes, and all men and women had access to the resources necessary for living. This indicates that inequality based on class and gender is not necessarily characteristic of human society. These observations are profound because they affirm the human potential for creating egalitarian, environmentally sustainable societies.

Rapa Nui

For most of human existence people moved from one place to another by walking, and the major continents were investigated by those who traveled on foot. Since the earth's surface is dominated by water, colonization of remote islands, which required sailing vessels and the capacity to navigate across expanses of water, took place at a far later time. Among the greatest navigators were the Polynesians, who colonized a huge surface area of the earth: the Hawaiian Islands in the north, New Zealand in the west, and Rapa Nui, better known as Easter Island, in the east. Because their sailing canoes could travel over 200 kilometers per day, and because they had learned how to preserve food for long periods of time, it was possible for them to sail 5,000 kilometers or more in a single voyage.

The culture that gave rise to the Polynesians is believed to have emerged in the Fiji-Tonga-Samoa area beginning about 1500 B.C.E. Soon thereafter Polynesians began their long period of expansion into the Pacific, reaching Rapa Nui around 400 C.E. (common era). No one knows for certain, but it is generally believed that few, if any, ever came or left the island after the original settlement by the people of the legendary chief Hotu Matu'a. This is not surprising since Rapa Nui is one of the most remote places ever permanently inhabited. The closest inhabited island is Pitcairn, which is 2,250 kilometers to the west. Rapa Nui's other close neighbors are Concepción, Chile, 3,747 kilometers to the east, and the Galapagos Islands, 3,872 kilometers to the north.

Hotu Matu'a's fabled landing at Anakena Beach on Rapa Nui brought the Polynesian settlers to a tropical paradise. Temperatures there range from about 23°C in the warmest months of January and February to about 18°C in the cool months of July and August. The island was ecologically stratified with grasslands along the coast, mixed trees and forest at elevations of 100 to 400 meters, and shrubs and grasses on the highest elevations. A giant palm that was a close relative to, or perhaps the same species as, the Chilean wine palm, *Jubaea chilensis,* once grew in abundance on Rapa Nui. The Chilean wine palm, the largest palm in the world, reaches heights of over 25 meters with a diameter of almost 2 meters. Its relative on Rapa Nui could provide the island's inhabitants with wood for seagoing boats and other building needs, as well as rollers for moving the giant *moai* (statues) for which Rapa Nui is noted. These early settlers used the toromiro tree's dense wood to build hot and long-burning fires and the hauhau bush's fibers to make excellent rope. Tree daisies along with shrubs, ferns, herbs, and grasses rounded out the island's flora. Although no mammals lived on Rapa Nui, at least 25 species of seabirds nested there, while more than 6 species of land birds made the island their home.

Rapa Nui is too far south for reef-forming corals to live, so the shoreline biological diversity is more limited than on reefed islands. Even so, the common porpoise and deep-sea fish could be hunted at sea from boats made from the palm tree. The soil was fertile, and the climate supported the growth of taro, yam, bananas, sweet potatoes, and sugar cane that arrived in Hotu Matu'a's canoes. The other standard Polynesian crops, breadfruit and coconut, could not be grown in the island's climate. Chickens and the Polynesian rat adapted well, while pigs and dogs, if they had made the trip, did not survive long. The biological diversity on the island and in the ocean around it ensured that food was plentiful and easily acquired.

On Easter afternoon in 1722, about 1,300 years after Rapa Nui was colonized by Polynesians, sailors on the first of three ships under the command of Dutch explorer Jacob Roggeveen spied what looked like a sandy, low, flat island. They gave it its European name, Easter Island. On the next day over 100 Dutch men, armed and in military formation, went ashore and proceeded to fire at least 30 muskets killing and wounding several Rapa Nui. The Dutch sailors took the supplies they needed and sailed away. We have no record from the Rapa Nui of these events, nor do we know how this encounter influenced their culture. The next reported European visit came almost 50 years later in 1770 with the arrival of a Spanish expedition under the command of Don Felipe Gonzalez de Haedo. The priests and soldiers put on a grand ceremonial show with banners, flags, drums, singing, a parade, rifle volleys, and a twenty-one-gun salute from the ships. They erected a cross on each of three prominent hills and claimed the island for Don Carlos of Spain. Four years later the Englishman Captain James Cook arrived with several persons who, unlike the people on the first European ships, had experience with Pacific islanders. They initiated the scientific investigations that would eventually explain what happened to Rapa Nui and the people who had come with Hotu Matu'a some 1,300 years earlier.

The entire island was a sea of grass essentially devoid of trees or shrubs. The largest native animals were insects — there were no birds or lizards or snails. The landscape was dominated by hundreds of stone *moai* ranging from 2 to 10 meters tall and weighing up to 82 tons. Hundreds more were in the quarries or on the roads leading from the quarries. The largest, El Gigante, 20 meters tall and weighing approximately 270 tons, lay in the quarry where it had been carved. About 2,000 people were living in thatch dwellings, or in caves, as a part of a society organized around warrior chiefs. The first Europeans had a difficult time imagining how these people with no timber, no rope, and only simple stone tools could have carved, moved, and erected the immense *moai.*

As we now know, Rapa Nui ancestors did carve, move, and erect the *moai* and *ahu,* a ceremonial stone structure with chambers and a platform on which *moai* were placed. Accomplishing these tasks required a culture that could sustain skilled carvers and engineers. When Polynesians arrived on Rapa Nui, they were accomplished boat builders, sailors, and agriculturists with well-established cultural traditions and beliefs. Their social structure was organized around chiefs who inherited their status and priests whose job it was to keep evil spirits and demons at bay and the gods pleased. The island presented new environmental circumstances

to the Polynesians, and there a culture formed whose powerful vision became embodied in *ahu* and *moai*. This culture's undergirding stories, beliefs, and rituals also provided the major elements that would propel it to disaster.

As the several dozen original colonizers adapted to the island, their numbers grew. From what is believed to have been two original clans, new groups formed and more of the island was settled. Forests were cleared for agriculture and for living and ceremonial spaces. The carving of *moai* began. Oceangoing boats were built to hunt porpoise, the main source of protein in their diet. All of these activities diminished the forests and their resources. Pollen analysis now shows that the forests were in decline by 800 C.E., but within any single human lifetime, the incremental changes would have gone unnoticed because the forests were extensive.

The bountiful resources of the sea and the land affirmed the Rapa Nui lifestyle and the relationships between its people and their gods. More *ahu* and *moai* must have seemed invaluable to the people of Rapa Nui to sustain themselves. Huge *moai* and *ahu* construction stones were moved from quarry to coastal erection sites, sometimes more than 10 kilometers, using palm logs as rollers. Over time the *moai* and *ahu* became larger and more complex, hinting at competition among groups. Population growth and statue construction now exerted unrelenting pressures on forests in general and on palms in particular. Unnoticed, the introduced Polynesian rat, whose sweet meat was a delicacy, made palm nuts part of its diet. This, coupled with the long germination time and slow growth of the palm seedling, meant that the palm forests were not renewing themselves at a rate compatible with their preservation, and they fell into decline. By 1400 C.E. the palm was extinct along with all the other species that required forest habitat.

The height of *moai* production coincided with the extinction of the palm, but the population peak, estimated between 6,000 and 10,000, did not occur until 1600 C.E., two hundred years later. When Europeans arrived, the population had fallen to about 2,000. The population peak and decline were associated with substantial social turmoil. The statue cult had been supplanted by the birdman cult, which coincided with the replacement of hereditary chiefs by warrior chiefs. The birdman cult was an elaborate ritual associated with the annual return of the sooty tern to the islet of Motu Nui, located 2 kilometers off the southern tip of Rapa Nui. Each warrior chief designate would climb down the 300-meter cliffs at Orongo, swim on a reed mat to Motu Nui, and await the arrival of the terns. The first man to collect a newly laid tern egg would swim back and present the egg to his warrior chief, and that chief would be the birdman for the next year. By the time this ritual began, no seabirds nested on Rapa Nui, nor did any land birds remain. The forests were gone, and the Rapa Nui people were truly marooned on a biologically impoverished island. This ritual worship of a living organism may have represented the beginnings of a cultural transformation that recognized the value of other life to human existence.

During this period of social turmoil the Rapa Nui apparently organized themselves into two groups who may have originated in the two clans of the original settlers. In the western alliance, the Miru possessed the highest status, which heralded back to Hotu Matu'a. From the mid 1400s to the early 1600s, in an effort to maintain the order and perhaps please the gods, a sequence of Miru chiefs exerted their authority to renovate the platform at Ahu Akivi and to erect seven *moai*. But, judging from the archaeological record, the island did not regain its former bounty. Porpoise bones disappeared from the Rapa Nui garbage heaps, and hundreds of stone chicken houses have been found, perhaps erected to preserve a family's source of protein. Obsidian, once used only for carving, was fashioned into daggers and spear points. Although the early European visitors reported seeing no weapons, they observed many wound scars on the natives. Bodies of the dead were hidden to prevent desecration. According to oral tradition, cannibalism was widespread, and human bones became common in trash heaps.

We will never know how the Rapa Nui people would have accommodated themselves to the biologically impoverished environment they had created or for how long they could have done so. The events associated with Easter Sunday in 1722, and those that followed, forever changed one of Polynesia's most fascinating cultures. The development of a culture, 1,300 years in the making, was interrupted.

Rapa Nui illustrates some essential points. First, massive environmental impoverishment does not require sophisticated technologies or modern market economies. When the scale and pattern of human use of biological resources outstrip the capacity for restoration, impoverishment eventually follows. Second, deleterious changes may be imperceptible from the perspective of an individual's life span, and this makes it difficult for any single generation to recognize its effects and take appropriate measures to ensure sustainability. Third, the time lag between the total loss of a life support system and the collapse of the culture can be long. On Rapa Nui the palm, and thus the forests, became extinct about 200 years before the population crashed and the statue culture totally disintegrated. Fourth, a culture's worldview can be very hard to change even when it is obviously dysfunctional.

The Greenland Norse

According to legend, Eric the Red chose the name Greenland to attract settlers. When permanent settlement began in 985 C.E. during an unusually warm period, the island's climate seemed similar to contemporary Scotland or Ireland, but it was an arctic ecosystem. The Norse established two settlements on Greenland, the Western and the Eastern Settlements, that persisted for 400 and 500 years, respectively. They brought with them Christian religious traditions and the farming and hierarchical social structure of northern Europeans. They grazed sheep, goats, and cattle on the fragile arctic grass ecosystem in the summer and fed them fodder in the winter. They ventured north in the summer to hunt caribou and seal pups for meat and walrus ivory for trade. Although they lived on the seashore, they did not fish. They built monumental cathedrals and in 1127 C.E. were sent their own bishop in exchange for a live polar bear and walrus ivory. Although Greenland was not well suited for European-style farming, the colonies grew to an estimated 6,000 inhabitants at their peak.

Although climate had been in a warm period when the Norse first came, beginning about 1300 C.E. the Little Ice Age settled in to cool the northern Atlantic. A series of chilly summers in the fourteenth century coincided with the disappearance of the settlers from the Western Settlement. The Norse in the Eastern Settlement persisted for another

100 years, but the members of this community also died out, and the settlement then ceased to exist. Their medieval-European culture had been permeated with Christian religious myths that moved them to build bigger and more ornate churches, but just as refurbishing *ahu* and *moai* on Rapa Nui did not bring back better times, cathedral construction did not reverse climate change.

In contrast, Thule hunters, ancestors of the contemporary Inuit who lived on Greenland with the Norse, continued to do well. No evidence has surfaced to indicate that conflict with the Thule caused the demise of the Norse. The Norse shunned heathen ways even though adopting some of them might have saved the settlements.

Archaeological excavations of the Western Settlement paint a depressing picture of the last years of that colony. Because of a string of cool summers, insufficient fodder was raised to feed its dairy cattle, which were slaughtered for food in violation of traditional Norse law. Near the end, even valuable elkhounds were butchered. The record of fly species found in bedroom floor sediments indicates a change from an indoor species that required warm quarters to two cold-tolerant indoor carrion species and then to a predominance of outdoor species in what was probably the last two years before the farm was abandoned. While the Thule hunted ringed-seals, the Norse shivered and killed their precious farm animals to stay alive. When their animals were gone, their farms and culture soon disappeared.

European style agriculture and culture were never appropriate for Greenland, even in the climatic warm period 1,000 years ago. Why did the Norse fail to see or learn this? Why did they perish instead of changing? Did constant European contact and trade continue to reinforce an inappropriate lifestyle? Did their myths prevent adaptive change? To believe that technology could overcome environmental limits and to refuse to change their social European pattern of habitation did not position the Norse to respond appropriately to climate change when it came. Contemporary global economic culture shares common cultural roots with the Norse. It is, therefore, reasonable to be concerned about global economic culture's ability to cope adaptively with biological and physical reality.

The Ladakhis

High in the Himalayas, just west of Tibet, two Aryan groups united with Mongolian nomads from Tibet to form the subsistence agricultural civilization of Ladakh. The early settlers were Buddhists, and their cultural beliefs were deeply influenced by this faith. Ladakhis understood that everything is connected. They believed it is impossible to see an object, an event, an idea, or a person as an isolated entity, because nothing exists in isolation; it is the connections that are important. Change is omnipresent, and everything changes or disappears. Life is a continuum of forms, so death is but a change of form. Only emptiness exists unchanging and unchangeable. Each thing can only be understood in relation to everything else. Spirits are everywhere and in everything and must be acknowledged and tended. All human action occurs within a completely interconnected universe in which humans are just an element.

Ladakh is a place of immense, stark beauty. The valleys begin at 3,000 meters above sea level and are surrounded by 6,000-meter-high snow-capped peaks that reach toward the sun. Some trees can grow at the lowest elevations, but scree and dust cover most of the land. The sun is intense and rain is rare, but glacial streams water the valleys. Although human habitation seems impossible in this fragile and biologically poor land, the Ladakhis have inhabited this land for 2,000 years. Their culture interacted well with the fragile ecosystems of these high elevations. Their pattern of habitation wasted nothing, and frugality meant a fruitful existence as they took their place in the ecosystem, recycling everything and polluting little.

The Ladakhi population was stable for centuries, and they understood and respected the limits of their mountain ecosystems. Although some families were large, custom ensured that an occasional large family did not lead to population growth. Many marriages were polyandrous, and a woman might have two or more husbands. Many unmarried women became Buddhist nuns, and although nuns could have children, they usually didn't. Some men became Buddhist monks, who were celibate, which resulted in even fewer families. In the end, a flexible pattern of individual decisions based on restrained behavior led to a stable population of around 100,000 in an area of 115,000 square kilometers.

Traditional Ladakhi agriculture is ecologically integrated and efficient. The main crop is barley, but wheat is planted in some areas. Peas and turnips are also cultivated in small plots. Wild plants, or weeds as industrialized agriculture would call them, that grow along paths or between fields fulfill myriad needs — *burtse,* fuel and animal fodder; *yagdzas,* roofing material; *tsermang,* fences; *demok,* red dye; and others, medicine and food. Apricot and walnut trees grow in valley orchards below 3,300 meters. At higher elevations, where barley will not grow, animals — sheep, goats, donkeys, horses, cows, yak, and a hybrid of the common cow and yak, the *dzo* — graze. The *dzo,* a large and strong but docile beast, is the draft animal of choice. At these elevations, the growing and grazing seasons are a short four months.

Agricultural land is individually owned and the average size is 5 acres. Some land also belongs to each monastery. The land is never divided but passes to the eldest son of the owner or, if a family has no sons, to the eldest daughter. Each family takes care of all of its members — children, parents, grandparents, and great-grandparents — from the products of its land, either directly or by trading. If a family has too many children to feed, the youngest son usually becomes a monk.

The Ladakhis are self-sufficient, trading with the outside world only for tea, salt, and the metals needed to make tools and cooking utensils. With only hand tools and simple technologies, a Ladakhi needs ample time to complete any task from start to finish. For example, making a wool coat requires raising the sheep, shearing them, cleaning, spinning, and weaving the wool into cloth, which is then cut and sewn to make the coat. Although all tasks take considerable time owing to the simple tools they use, the Ladakhis do not rush and live leisurely lives. Indeed, they only work consistently during the four-month growing season. In winter the animals must be fed, water carried, and meals prepared, but parties and festivals occupy much of the time.

An active life at elevations over 3,000 meters, in combination with a simple diet of native foods, makes the Ladakhis a robust and trim people with few health problems aside from the usual digestive disorders, respiratory infections, and common skin and eye problems. Because of the bitterly cold winters, where -40°C is not unusual, the first year of life is precarious, and infant mortality is high. Once past the first year, many live into their seventies, usually active right up to the time of death. The *amchi,* or doctor, is trained in the holistic, Tibetan system of medicine. In the Buddhist tradition, illness is not seen as an isolated phenomenon but as connected to the whole person and all of his or her existence. Hundreds of natural compounds are employed for their medicinal properties, which might remind us that well over half of drug store medicines originate in a plant, animal, or microbe.

Ladakhis sing constantly. Every activity has its songs, and everybody knows the songs and sings them. Few tasks are done alone; and work is not separated from socializing. Activities form a continuum in which all members from young children to aging adults participate. In each village everybody knows everybody else. Virtually all economic exchanges take place within and among households, and since households are self-sufficient, almost all decisions are made at household level. The few village-level decisions are made democratically by small groups of households and their representatives.

Many Ladakhi traditions, or patterns of living, have been created to make it possible for people to live together with minimal conflict. To be called a *schon chan,* "one who angers easily," is to receive perhaps the strongest insult possible in Ladakh. If a man's wife is having an affair, anger is not the appropriate response, for then he would have committed the greater offense. His response in this situation, as in many others that might result in an angry conflict in industrialized culture, would be, *chi choen?* "what's the point?" The situation is acknowledged and a resolution emerges. Often, when an interaction with potential conflict arises, or a negotiation is to be made, a third party resolves the conflict or participates in the negotiation. This third party might even be a stranger but is respected as though the arrangement had been preplanned. The ideal is for everybody to live together well in as fair and equitable a fashion as possible. It worked for a long time.

Although India built a military road to Ladakh and stationed troops there when China invaded and occupied Tibet, it wasn't until the mid 1970s that the Indian government decided that Ladakh offered great promise for the tourist industry. Spectacularly beautiful, remote, and containing an almost undisturbed traditional subsistence culture, Ladakh was exactly what tourists coveted. Guides were needed, and roads, accommodations, and restaurants were built. A money economy was imposed, supplementing the traditional barter system. Materials and technologies flowed into the major towns and then into the remote villages that had, for all practical purposes, been isolated for centuries.

Ladakh is changing. The population is growing beyond what can be supported. The Indian government now requires Ladakhi children to be educated as children are in the industrial world. Young people are now often ashamed of traditional ways. They have heard spectacular professional singers who are much better singers than they are. With this knowledge and self-consciousness some Ladakhis are now embarrassed to sing while they work and singing is less common now. They covet material things and experiences that require money, so they seek jobs outside the villages. The old beliefs and values are no longer central to everybody's existence.

Ladakhis have always understood that nothing is permanent and that everything is in a state of change. Now, a kind of change never experienced in traditional Ladakhi culture has come to the serene land of mountain passes and high desert valleys, and these changes have very different origins than the culture that sustained Ladakhi civilization for thousands of years. Ladakhis now confront the immense challenge that all humans face: can contemporary societies create patterns of sustainable habitation on a local level that are compatible with global markets where money can substitute for anything and the exchange of almost everything can occur at the speed of light?

Nauru's traditional culture and those of the Australian aborigines, Kalahari !Kung, Rapa Nui, Greenland Norse, and Ladakhis are but a small sample of the immense human cultural diversity that has emerged on Earth. Every human culture has a long history reflecting the many physical, biological, and social environments it has experienced and the countless choices its members have made. This cultural lineage is similar to the deep evolutionary history of a species or an ecosystem. In all three — species, ecosystem, and culture — a profound intertwining among genes and environments has molded what has persisted. For a species the memory of past environments has primarily been written in the genes, while for ecosystems and cultures the imprinting of history is found at other levels of interaction as well. Every ecosystem is a record of past and present species and their relations, while each culture is a record of a people's responses to their changing environments, including inter-actions with other cultures. Species, ecosystems, and cultures are irre-placeable yet ephemeral. The future will be populated by species, ecosys-tems, and cultures that have adapted to the biological and physical conditions they have experienced.

Chapter Five

Science as Story

For 10,000 years, all but a remnant handful of hunting-gathering societies have been living outside the normal, local-ecosystem confines of nature. That is why our cultural heritage proclaims us to be something apart from, even over and above, the beasts of the field. We need an updated story, one that acknowledges that we did not so much leave the natural world as redefine our position in it.

NILES ELDREDGE, *Dominion*

THE AUSTRALIAN ABORIGINES, the Kalahari !Kung, the Nauruans, and the Ladakhis lived socially and spiritually rich lives for thousands of years. Individuals within these groups were secure as members of a society in which people took care of each other. Their social systems maintained populations below the carrying capacities of the areas where they lived. Most of their time was spent socializing and performing rituals that connected them to their place and to each other. In contrast, the Rapa Nui and the Greenland Norse — and many other cultures — failed to live according to the biological and physical constraints of their habitats and hence degraded their local environments. In these cultures, humans eventually exceeded the capacity of their ecosystems to support their pattern of living. These peoples — and others — did not perceive, or effectively respond to, the negative balances in their ecological books. In addition, many peoples had degraded their environments so much that they no longer had the resources to respond to sudden environmental change. Their technologies no longer could overcome resource constraints, and so their civilizations collapsed and often disappeared.

Hunter-gatherer societies in general, and subsistence agricultural cultures such as those of Nauru and Ladakh, show that people can live well without irreversibly degrading their environment. The patterns of habitation of numerous gatherers and hunters were sustainable because these humans were just one of the many large animals that lived, in small numbers, from the sun's energy flow. They employed simple tools and technologies and used fire to modify vegetation and to hunt game, but they altered the environment little more than other animals such as army ants, beavers, or elephants. The effect of their habitation on the environment was mainly local, and most such effects were accommodated by natural processes. For most of human existence people lived under the same constraints that other large animals did.

Where humans developed and adopted agriculture as a means of acquiring food, population rose, permanent settlements became the norm, social stratification became pronounced, and humans dramatically increased their capacity to alter and damage local ecosystems. Indeed, agriculture usually replaces stable, highly evolved ecosystems with unstable, simple ones. The history of agricultural societies chronicles great losses to biological diversity and many instances of reduced soil fertility, followed by crop failures and cultural dysfunction and collapse. In already impoverished and stressed ecosystems, climate change often caused crop failures. The traditional cultures on Nauru and in Ladakh, among other agricultural societies, reveal that agriculture per se is not the reason for unsustainable habitation, yet it certainly does tilt the balance in favor of disruptive practices that predispose a culture to instability, especially in light of the positive feedback loops common to population growth and agriculture. In other words, surplus food promotes a larger population, and in turn a larger population encourages the production of more food.

Why were traditional Nauruan and Ladakhi cultures sustainable even though they practiced agriculture? The unique circumstances on Nauru and in the Himalayas must have been critical to the creation and duration of these sustainable cultures. Neither Ladakh or Nauru was well endowed with biological diversity, nor was either climate ideal for human habitation. On the contrary, when compared to a place like Rapa Nui or parts of Europe and North America, each was poor biologically and its climate harsh. Nauru was almost always hot, and the island routinely experienced mild-to-severe droughts. Ladakh had little rainfall, and conditions above 3,000 meters were difficult — a short growing season followed by very cold temperatures during the rest of the year. These severe conditions gave the Ladakhi agriculturalists little flexibility. The lag time between environmental abuse and negative feedback must have been short, and the Ladakhis apparently responded quickly to this feedback. They did not have the luxury of time, as did the Rapa Nui, who realized only too late the consequences of hundreds of years of overuse of their forests. Perhaps the fragility of the Ladakhis' life-support systems sensitized them to their precarious existence — an understanding they embodied in their cultural beliefs and patterns of living.

Scale is another significant factor that appears correlated to the sustainability of an agricultural society. Nauru was small, and Ladakh, though covering a substantial land area, operated politically and economically in groups of fewer than 100 people. The intimacy afforded by the nature of their social, political, and economic systems may have enabled these cultures to respond in timely fashion to feedback from their fragile ecosystems.

As Western culture developed, it encountered many challenging but also rich and resilient ecosystems. Despite their continent's great resources, during much of the last 1,000 years most Europeans were undernourished, disease-ridden peasants who were pawns in violent conflicts among the religious, hereditary, political, and military elites. Although some local environmental degradation occurred in Europe, its peoples' expansion into the rest of the world, beginning about 500 years ago, prevented overpopulation and environmental destruction from exacting a greater toll. By exporting their excess population and importing materials from the rest of the world, Europeans temporarily evaded the limitations of their local ecosystems.

It was only in the twentieth century that the fruits of several hundred years of Western science, technology, and imperialism made life in Europe healthier, physically easier, and materially rich for the many who had access to this new wealth. From the perspective of recent history, the conditions for Westerners have greatly improved; however, from a longer view, this improvement is really just a reversal of thousands of years of worsening conditions. In the twentieth century, the height and life span of the average European — after adjusting for infant mortality — equaled once again those found 15,000–20,000 years ago among gatherers and hunters of prehistoric Europe.

Twentieth-century technological accomplishments would have been inconceivable to travelers from European ports at the beginning of the Renaissance: transportation to anywhere in the world within about a day, men walking on the moon, cures for many diseases and the elimination of others, instantaneous transmission of voice and image to anywhere on the planet, transplantation of human kidneys and hearts, the capacity of one person to provide food for fifty, and the ability to live almost anywhere on earth in comfort. Although these advances took the better part of 10,000 years, during which life for many was "nasty, brutish, and short," most see such accomplishments as clear indications that Western culture has manifested its mythical birthright by its purported mastery over earth's land and creatures.

Other things, however, have also been happening. Burning immense amounts of fossil fuels and eliminating huge areas of forest have contributed significantly to the 30 percent increase in atmospheric carbon dioxide concentration recorded in just the last 100 years. Almost all scientists who study the influence of greenhouse gases on climate have concluded that the earth's climate will change substantially as a consequence of our continuing alteration of the atmosphere. Human-made chemical compounds are thinning the stratospheric ozone layer that shields the earth's surface from dangerous ultraviolet rays. Exotic chemicals, like chlorinated hydrocarbons and others that mimic hormones, are changing life in unpredictable and harmful ways. Scientists have evidence that hormone mimics cause gross birth defects, decreased fertility, behavioral abnormalities, feminization of males and masculinization of females, and immune system dysfunctions in many populations of wild animals. Soils are eroding many times faster than they are forming, and agricultural output has been maintained only by huge infusions of chemically synthesized fertilizers. Most of the ocean's fisheries are in decline, and some are completely fished out. The rates of ecosystem and habitat destruction are accelerating. The sixth mass species extinction of the past 600 million years is well under way. These disasters, the by-products of humanity's fantastic technological achievements and the immense size of the human population, are negative feedback signals from the earth's life-support systems. On a planetary scale they are analogous to the signals that came quickly on Nauru and in Ladakh but slowly and fatally on Rapa Nui. If our global civilization is to persist, we must heed these signals in time.

Science and technology have given the world not only the capacity to alter biological and physical processes on a global scale but also an understanding of how the universe began and how Earth came to be covered with the incredible diversity of life of which we are a part. The concepts and understandings provided by natural scientists — most notably Copernicus and Galileo, and then Darwin and Wallace — seriously challenge Western culture's biblical creation story. Because of the creativity of these thinkers and thousands of others, the natural sciences have given us a new story of how the world and humans came to be the way they are.

World economic culture is presently in the stressful throes of transforming its archaic, and now unbelievable, mythological base. The impetus for this transformation is the scientific explanation of physical and biological reality. We recount this story in some detail, because it is as inspirational as any explanation the world has known. More important, however, it creates a rationale for replacing nonadaptive myths about the purpose of human existence with alternatives that could lead to a new way for humans to live in harmony with the rest of creation.

The story of how humans came into existence begins with the birth of the universe some 12 billion years ago. More than half of known time passed before our solar system and Earth were formed. Within a billion years of Earth's formation, life evolved and our planet's biotic enterprise began in earnest. Bacterialike organisms spread across Earth's surface and, over the eons, profoundly changed the planet. Several hundred million years after they first appeared on Earth, bacteria evolved a phenomenally liberating process — photosynthesis. Life was no longer dependent upon the random, inefficient geological and chemical processes that had until then provided energy to power life processes. Photosynthesis efficiently and directly provided cells with an endless supply of energy from the sun, and this process would radically change the course of Earth's evolutionary venture.

Photosynthesis not only combined water and carbon dioxide to make carbohydrates — life's energy coinage — but also released oxygen into a world whose ancient atmosphere lacked oxygen. But the oxygen did not appreciably accumulate in the atmosphere for a long time. Most of the photosynthetically released oxygen was quickly used by resident bacteria to convert photosynthetically produced carbohydrates back to water, carbon dioxide, and metabolic energy. Enormous quantities of soluble iron in the ocean also combined with released oxygen to form insoluble iron oxide, which settled to the bottom. It took over a billion years before the oceans' iron was removed, and vast quantities of photosynthetically produced carbohydrates were buried in ocean sediments, thereby enabling the oxygen released by photosynthesis to accumulate in the atmosphere to substantial levels. The new oxygenated atmosphere was toxic to most early life, killing much of the bacterial diversity that evolved in earth's original oxygen-free atmosphere. This mass extinction, perhaps the first, was surely slow but relentless.

Out of the ooze and turmoil of 2 billion years of bacterial life, another cell type evolved by the symbiotic association of several bacterial cell types. This spectacular creation, the eukaryotic cell, contained organelles that enabled cellular functions to take place in locations separated by membranes. The nucleus contained most of the cell's genetic information, and the mitochondrion became the organelle for aerobic energy release — the energy transformer that would provide unprecedented power for fantastic biological adventures. In the eukaryotic cell type that evolved into algae, the chloroplast became the organelle that housed pigments and other components required for photosynthesis. These new cell types created opportunities for stunning, glorious diversity.

The universe continued to expand, and the earth's rotation, which had an initial period of less than 18 hours, slowed over billions of years to our current 24-hour day. New patterns of biological diversity appeared. The organisms with adaptive patterns survived, while those without such patterns left no descendants. From a billion to 600 million years ago, many kinds of multicellular organisms evolved, and a surge of new life filled the oceans. Some of these wonderful creatures commenced a journey onto the land. Although from the earliest times bacteria may have existed there, until this period the land would have been unable to sustain water-born multicellular life.

Plants — evolutionarily separated from animals almost a billion years earlier — were the first to undertake this remarkable evolutionary adventure to overcome the obstacles to living beyond the water-limited world. A hydraulic skeleton created by internal water pressure against the cell wall provided a means of support in the absence of water's natural buoyancy, and waterproof cuticle conserved water when it no longer enveloped these organisms. As the plants created new habitats and provided rich sources of food on the land, invertebrates quickly evolved to pursue the plants. Three hundred million years ago insects, the land's most abundant animals, created myriad niches and dominated the earth, as they still do. Vertebrates, however, would need far more time to create

their niches on land. As illogical as it may seem to us, evolution dictated that our vertebrate ancestors first brave the land to survive in water — not to colonize the land.

A group of freshwater fish had evolved an accessory lung that enabled them to breathe air when their water environment became so stagnant and oxygen-depleted that fish without this lung died. The new lung, although primitive, enabled them to breathe air as they dragged themselves on stumpy fins from one stagnant puddle to another. From this modest beginning, the vertebrate lineage moved onto the land and evolved into an array of organisms — first amphibians and then reptiles.

The earth's continents are always moving, colliding and separating. Molten magma below the crust is constantly vented to the surface. Asteroids and comets have buffeted the earth. And every once in a while an enormous object collides with the earth, literally shaking it. In fact, our moon is a piece of Earth knocked free by a gigantic impact early in the planet's history. These and other activities change the climate locally and, at times, globally. Over the long haul the vast diversity of earth's multicellular organisms has enabled that vein of the biotic enterprise to survive and flourish in the face of constant and occasionally dramatic environmental change. Nevertheless, this richness of multicellular biological diversity has suffered monumental losses. Because the fossil record does not establish an organism's metabolism or other characteristics employed to classify an organism precisely, we know far less about the microorganisms — viruses, bacteria, protozoans, and fungi — but their biological diversity also enabled them to survive the same events that affected multicellular species.

Four hundred and seventy million years ago, the earth's continents were united in one supercontinent called Pangea I. Over the next two hundred and twenty million years the continents separated and then came together again, forming another giant land mass, Pangea II. As the continents drifted together to form Pangea II, local and global climates changed substantially. The colliding continents apparently triggered intense volcanic activity. Many habitats changed, while others disappeared because of climate variations and the reconfiguration of land masses. These changes resulted in the earth's largest mass extinction of multicellular life, which is known as the Great Dying, dated 250 million years ago. Some scientists hypothesize that a substantial increase of carbon dioxide in the oceans resulted in the Great Dying, but its causes remain uncertain.

Although the causes are still debated, we do know that many forms of life were decimated; and in some taxonomic groups, like the marine invertebrates, up to 96 percent of the species disappeared. Among the surviving species, an evolutionary race ensued to determine which vertebrate group would dominate the land. The ancestors of the dinosaurs won and gave rise to that group. With hundreds of dinosaur species occupying the dominant ecological niches for more than 150 million years, our ancestors, the mammals, were kept in the shadows. A successful organism is not easily displaced, unless environmental change subjects the organism to new selection pressure. When the changes are sufficient and the selection pressure is great enough, extinction often follows. With extinction of some species, new evolutionary possibilities emerge for other species; however, the extinction of some and the survival and evolution of others to fill newly available ecological space seems haphazard.

If a controlling intelligence is responsible for ordering life, it is indiscernible in the chaotic processes that weave the fabric of life.

Sixty-five million years ago, a meteorite 10 kilometers in diameter rammed the earth near the Yucatán Peninsula and left a crater 190 kilometers wide. The low angle of impact apparently caused a firestorm that incinerated much of western North America in a matter of hours and touched off a tsunami that reached the southern Great Plains. The atmosphere filled with debris, and the earth's surface darkened for months, perhaps years. Plants died; animals starved. Particularly vulnerable were the carnivores at the top of the food chain and large herbivores that required constant and substantial energy from photosynthesis. For the dinosaurs, some of which may have already been in decline for several million years, the climate changes and the selection pressures wrought by the meteorite dealt the death blow. Within a short time all dinosaurs, except the lineage leading to the birds, were extinct.

The vertebrates of the terrestrial world were again decimated, as they had been 185 million years earlier. This time the mammals, whose ecological roles had long been limited by the domination of the dinosaurs, inherited the land, an empty landscape offering great opportunities for species evolution. A plethora of mammals filled the continents. Some ventured back into the water, while others took to the air. The climate continued to change, and coupled with geological events, these changes fueled widespread speciation. Two to three million years ago, in what is now called Africa a branch of the primate line spawned a new genus, *Homo,* from which several species emerged. These species walked upright, had large brains in comparison with most other animals, and manipulated their environment in unique ways. Some of the first *Homo* species walked out of Africa to gather, hunt, and scavenge food in other continents.

Several hundred thousand years ago our species, *Homo sapiens,* evolved on the savannas of Africa. These ancestors of ours had a brain even larger than earlier *Homo* species and a growing capacity to communicate, make tools, and manipulate the environment. Like earlier humans, this new species moved out of Africa and walked across the earth in small bands; as they went, they adapted culturally, and to a lesser extent genetically, to local habitats. They probably interacted with other *Homo* species and subspecies, but exactly how is unclear. The outcome of these interactions, though, is known: the *Homo sapiens* that spread from Africa within the last several hundred thousand years is now the only surviving *Homo* species on the planet.

For 100,000 years or more our species lived in small bands gathering, scavenging, and occasionally hunting within the boundaries of the ecosystems they inhabited. Many patterns of culture evolved among the thousands upon thousands of gatherer-hunter-scavenger bands that inhabited the planet. Again the forces of change are uncertain, but beginning about 10,000 years ago, perhaps because of climate change and population pressure, some groups initiated agriculture in disparate places around the globe, and this was followed, and in other cases preceded, by domestication of plants and animals to obtain food. Domestication brought the reproduction of these plants and animals under control, and hence the evolution of domesticated species became human directed. We can see the result in gardens — for example, broccoli, cauliflower, brussels sprouts, cabbage, and other seemingly different plants are all the same species, *Brassica oleracea* — or among dogs, whose myriad breeds, including Chihuahuas, Great Danes, and poodles, are all the same species, *Canis familiaris*.

In association with other changes in our culture, agriculture profoundly altered how we interacted with the ecosystems we inhabited and with each other. The number of people who lived in close proximity rose substantially. Institutionalized religions, cities, social hierarchies, labor specialization, and organized, large-scale conflict — all had their beginnings in the advent of agriculture and domestication. In many places the jump in the number of people, coupled with the new patterns of habitation, enabled humans to alter ecosystems as never before.

Agriculture and population growth reinforced each other; population skyrocketed locally and globally. The technology that included irrigation, the wheel, the plow, the yoke, and improved methods of crop rotation made agriculture more productive. These tools and methods were also the harbingers of the Western technological civilization that fermented in Europe and that over the past thousand years has infiltrated all the world's cultures.

After several hundred years of intensive scientific inquiry, we understand the facts, albeit incompletely, about the biological realities of who we are and where we came from. After a long caravan of human generations, we know that we are one of the millions of species that have evolved on this speck of rock in a boundless universe. This knowledge has been hard won, and as a science story, it will always be in the making. This empirically verified scientific creation story replaces those that have told us that we are "chosen" creatures, immune from the natural laws that apply to all species.

Although scientists and others have shown that many of the central beliefs and values that undergird modern industrialized culture are inconsistent with sustainable patterns of living, science itself is deeply embedded in this culture. As it has developed and been used over the past several hundred years, science has empowered the industrial market culture to do exactly what it has been doing, as exemplified on Nauru and elsewhere. Science, however, can also guide us along another path. Our current path will no doubt lead to the demise of our civilization and its global market culture, while another road may bring us to adopt sustainable patterns of living as observed in traditional Nauruan and Ladakhi cultures, or among the !Kung and Australian aborigines.

Science as commonly practiced has been relatively objective and primarily driven by the scientific cultural value of ferreting out what is not true and discovering what might be true. At the same time, scientific culture is deeply embedded in the larger culture, which ascribes values to the findings of science. Scientists themselves often play a central role in this valuing. The interactions among scientists and the larger culture are exemplified in genetic engineering, where biologists have made it possible to move a gene from one organism — virus, bacterium, fungus, plant, or animal, including a human — into another organism and have it function to correct a defect or give the recipient organism new capabilities. This reality is often interpreted to mean that all living things are just machines and that, like auto mechanics, biologists successfully isolate fundamental parts and move them from one organism to another. As with the clockwork metaphor of the solar system, the metaphor of organic machines may indicate a scientific truth; however, we must remind ourselves that this very metaphor is culturally conditioned. Shall we continue to reduce everything, including humans, to machines, or shall we exalt everything — wind, water, trees, rocks, and people — as if all had spirits, as some of our ancestors believed?

Physicists, chemists, and biologists offer ways to explain reality that obviate the need for the spirits in which ancient peoples believed. For most modern people the idea that humans exist without spirits or souls is hard to accept, yet if we trust scientific explanations of how the world works, it is difficult to believe that people are sacred or spirited while the rest of the universe is not. Biologists have established that the fundamental unit of life is the cell — all life is composed of one or more of them — and every cell springs from a preexisting one. Although all of the wondrous properties of life emerge and become possible with the formulation of a cell, the cell is special only because of its organization, so if we seek spirits or enchantment, they will not mysteriously manifest themselves as an emergent property of cellular organization. Rather, they will appear, as ancient peoples believed, at all levels of organization: from elementary particles identified by physicists to molecular interactions worked out by chemists to plate tectonics discovered by geologists to organisms, ecosystems, and biomes described by biologists and to human societies analyzed by anthropologists, artists, economists, historians, philosophers, sociologists, and theologians. Our curiosity expressed in science has led us once again to the realization that we are an integral part of a fascinating and sacred universe. Our attention is turned away from a narrow human focus to embrace the whole world and even the universe beyond.

For more than a century, results from investigations in the natural sciences have supported the view that we are not separate from but an inextricable part of earth's biotic adventure. This understanding is similar to those of preceding cultures that created durable relations with their surroundings. We now realize that biological and physical reality is snuffing out our expansionary pattern of living of the past several thousand years. We are beginning to challenge and change our deep beliefs about the purpose of human existence, but we must also alter our patterns of living to preserve the biotic richness on which we utterly depend and which is under relentless attack.

Chapter Six

To Love a Cockroach

It is a matter of great concern in thinking about the global ecosystem to reflect that the packing of organisms, the communities that humans evolved into, and the communities in which they formulated and developed agriculture only about ten thousand years ago, were biologically the most complex communities that had ever existed on land. When we human beings try to replace those systems with others that are more directly focused on the kind of productivity that we want, we are modifying enormously complex systems about which we know next to nothing and which we have been studying seriously for only a few decades in the half million years of our history, and the 4.5 billion years of Earth history.

PETER RAVEN, *Environmental Review*

BEFORE 1800, NAURUANS depended on the island's biological diversity for their existence. If the coconut palm had become extinct during this time, the Nauruans would have had to rely on pandanus fruits, *ibija* fish, coral reef resources, and other plants and animals; and the loss of this source of vitamin B1 could have been devastating. If the coral reef had died, its fish and other organisms would have vanished, eliminating an essential source of protein. If insects and other animals that pollinated the island's flowering plants had disappeared, many plants would have become extinct — another disaster for the Nauruans. If bacteria, fungi, insects, and other invertebrates in the soil that supplied nutrients to plants had died, all plants would have perished and human life on the island would have been impossible.

Like Nauruans before 1800, contemporary peoples everywhere are threads in the web of life, which is woven into a fabric of innumerable other threads. This living fabric — the biosphere — is what makes Earth a comfortable, habitable place for us. In order to thrive, every human being needs exactly what this fabric provides. To appreciate this reality, try a simple thought experiment: Imagine you are alone in a remote place. Now make a list of the things you will need to thrive:

First, you will very quickly die without oxygen, an essential of human life that has its source in biological processes. With the help of the sun's energy, green plants break the chemical bonds in water and produce oxygen as a by-product. Oxygen must be maintained at about 21 percent of the atmosphere because substantially higher concentrations will burn human tissues and all other forms of life and because lower concentrations don't provide enough oxygen to keep human beings active or healthy. To maintain oxygen concentration at a consistent 21 percent requires a wide range of organisms — photosynthetic bacteria, algae, ferns, gymnosperms, numerous flowering plants and all of the bacteria, fungi, insects, and other animals these plants require to complete their life cycles.

External heat too is a requirement for human life, and you will freeze without heat, even in the tropics. To retain heat your remote place needs an atmosphere that admits the sun's light energy and traps some of it as heat. Again, as with human oxygen needs, humans require just the right amount of heat because cellular biochemistry falters and then fails outside the temperature range of 0°C to 100°C, that is, from the freezing point to the boiling point of water. The human metabolism, as with those of most other organisms, operates in a narrow temperature band between these extremes. If a human being's core body temperature deviates much from 37°C, he or she is in big trouble: at above 40°C or below 34°C brain metabolism falters, homeostasis cannot be maintained, and death follows. Again, the processes maintaining an atmosphere at appropriate surface temperatures involve many organisms. Water vapor and carbon dioxide are major greenhouse gases that make earth habitable. Plants transpire vast quantities of water into the air and via photosynthesis remove tons of carbon dioxide. Most organisms respire carbon dioxide as they use energy to stay alive. The heat retention of bare ground, grassy field, or forest is different from each other. These and other organism-dependent processes make major contributions to the maintenance of livable temperatures.

And you won't survive long without a source of energy, because an energy source is equally essential to human survival, and like oxygen and heat, this derives from organism-dependent processes. Plants convert and store some of the sun's energy in compounds such as carbohydrates and fats that human beings can metabolize for energy. Many plants require insects and other organisms to pollinate their flowers so they can reproduce and make food that can be consumed by humans. Human cells cannot synthesize all 20 amino acids necessary to make proteins (major structural components of cells and tissues, as well as the catalysts of metabolism); for that, we need plant or animal tissues that have sufficient concentrations of these essential amino acids. We depend on animals for their muscle tissues or for other products like milk as amino acid sources, and in turn, animals must have other animals or plants to eat. Our bodies can't make all of the required vitamins; we need bacteria in our intestines to make some vitamins, and we must eat various organisms to obtain other vitamins. We also use medicines to stay healthy, most of which come from microorganisms, plants, and animals.

Our bodies are over 90 percent water, and temperature maintenance, as well as waste removal, requires substantial amounts of water. We can live weeks without food but only days without water. Thus, we must have a supply of drinkable water, whose source may be the forests and wetlands that do an excellent job of retaining and purifying water.

After we eat and drink, we create waste products. Other animals produce wastes also, and plants and other organisms pile up along with these wastes. Bacteria, fungi, insects, and other invertebrates recycle these materials, which provide the chemical building blocks for new organisms. We are utterly dependent on other life forms and their intricate associations for basic sustenance.

Although your physical needs may be fulfilled, what about your emotional and spiritual ones? Even if it were possible to live in a barren place without other life, it would not be pleasant. Green plants are pleasing to see, and their presence is emotionally calming and beneficial. Interacting with animals can satisfy many human emotional needs. Fascination, inspiration, kindness, compassion, anxiety, wonder, apprehension, curiosity, dread, and fear — all are elicited by one organism or another. These and other emotional responses evoked by life around us appear essential to our mental health. Spiritual affiliations with other organisms are legion in human history; the very essence of human spirituality is intimately associated with other life forms. And, of course, we need a host of other humans — varied and diverse in talent and character.

Each organism lives interdependently with many others, and each must have its needs met. Like a human being, each is associated with other organisms in a habitat where there are amenable physical and chemical conditions. Habitats are located in ecosystems characterized as physical spaces defined by the presence of a species or by a physical boundary, like an oak-hickory forest, a sedge meadow, a pond, or a rotting log. An ecosystem includes all nonliving and living things that occupy the space.

The biological resources — as well as the knowledge and information — required to satisfy your physical, emotional, and spiritual needs are many and complex in an assemblage of ecosystems inherently diverse enough to sustain human life. Seven years of planning by a team of scientists and engineers led in 1991 to the creation in the Arizona desert of Biosphere 2, an artificial, mostly self-contained, scaled-down model of various ecosystems on earth. The enclosed model covered 1.25 hectares of several intact ecosystems: tropical rain forest, desert, coral reef, mangrove swamp, cattail marsh, and grassy savanna. The original goal was to demonstrate that eight adults, men and women, could live isolated in Biosphere 2 for two years.

Soon after the air locks were sealed, the oxygen concentration dropped from 21 to 15 percent and the carbon dioxide concentration began to rise. The concentration jumped seven times above the normal level at night when all organisms were respiring, and carbon dioxide was three times above normal in the day when the plants were consuming carbon dioxide through photosynthesis. To reduce carbon dioxide production, plant materials were not composted and rainfall on the desert was tripled to increase plant productivity. Savanna grasses then began growing in the desert, which in turn led to the extinction of some desert species. In the end, those in charge resorted to nonbiological means to remove carbon dioxide and add oxygen to Biosphere 2.

When many of the insects died, the residents hand-pollinated the plants required for fruit and seed production. The insects that survived, among them cockroaches and ants, damaged the garden and caused other problems. On average, each Biospherian lost 25 pounds over the two-year period. Although Biosphere 2 was a worthwhile experiment for testing our capacity to create a livable habitat, the inhabitants and their model failed to accomplish what planet Earth does without any help from us.

Biosphere 2 demonstrated that the earth's biosphere is incredibly delicate and that conditions suitable for humans and other organisms are very specific. Our biosphere is like a self-regulating and durable superorganism; it works extremely well on its own to make Earth not only a wonderful place but also the only place where humans can live for any period of time. Biosphere 2, as well as experiments with humans in spacecraft or inhospitable places on earth, confirms that living permanently in a highly simplified world would be unpleasant, essentially unworkable, and an inappropriate idea to entertain seriously. These experiments also illustrate that the biological diversity that permits a materially and spiritually rich human existence is more than a collection of individual species; rather, the biological diversity that nurtures human existence is an endless exchange feeding on itself. It encompasses essentially all species currently on earth and the variations within each species — all interacting among themselves and the constituents of their environments.

Although people often refer to the number of species as biological diversity or biodiversity, these terms include all levels of biological organization from the molecular to the biospheric. Biodiversity makes Earth different from every other place we know of in our solar system and in the universe. Venus, Mars, Saturn, and Jupiter's moons, for example, have physical processes, chemical processes, and geological processes, but as far as scientists know, they do not have biological processes. Because of the endless array of stars, we assume other places in the universe have planets with life, but we do not know for certain.

Humans need biodiversity; however, human activities worldwide are unequivocally responsible for altering the biosphere and reducing biodiversity as significantly as the asteroid did when it slammed into the planet 65 million years ago. Perhaps the clearest evidence of this phenomenon is that humans have, in a short time, appropriated a large fraction of the earth's ecological space at the expense of many other organisms and ecosystems. Nevertheless, many people are unaware of the human-caused mass extinction of species, or they believe it is merely a controversial opinion advocated by extremists.

While attempting to assess the magnitude of species loss and bearing in mind that the task of acquiring information and making assessments is forbidding, we must question why we have failed to collect and assess the information for such an all-important matter. Perhaps one reason for this failure derives from a traditional Western view that ignores or downgrades the importance of biodiversity. Another is more technical: scientists lack enough data to assemble a comprehensive record of species loss with any degree of precision. To establish dates of mass extinctions, we must know when exceptionally large numbers of species ceased to exist. To determine the normal, or "background rates," of species extinction, we need to know how long a typical species of a larger category of organisms — like a bird, a fish, or a mammal — survived, that is, the time between the species' appearance and disappearance. Such information on extinction is obtained by examining the fossil record. Problems arise because many organisms do not leave fossils, and those that do often have incomplete records. The fossils also must be of sufficient quality for paleontologists to narrow down their taxonomic level: kingdom, phylum, class, order, family, genus, species. To determine a species' extinction with certainty, fossils must be identified at the species level. Also, fossils from a species' geographic range must be available to measure its longevity. Despite such technical problems and others, we do have enough data to know when mass extinctions occurred and to estimate species extinction rates prior to the appearance of humans.

Fossils are most often made when an organism becomes embedded in sediments. The best and most comprehensive worldwide fossil records are available for marine invertebrates because they lived primarily where sediments were continuously deposited and because vast expanses of marine sedimentary rock are available for examination. These marine invertebrate records, complemented by those of other types of organisms, indicate five mass extinctions of multicellular organisms: 440 million years ago (MYA) at the end of the Ordovician period, 365 MYA near the end of the Devonian period, 250 MYA at the end of the Permian period, 210 MYA in the middle of the Triassic period, and 65 MYA at the end of the Cretaceous period.

Because it is often difficult to classify fossils at the species level, extinctions are usually categorized at a higher taxonomic level such as genus or family. During each of the mass extinctions over 15 percent of marine invertebrate families became extinct, except in the Permian extinction, during which about 54 percent of families were lost. Since many species in a family die out before the entire family becomes extinct, the percent of extinct species usually exceeds that of extinct families. In the great Permian extinction, for example, between 77 to 96 percent of all invertebrate marine species became extinct. Not all organisms suffered similar losses during these episodes. The most vulnerable were carnivores high on a food chain or organisms associated with fragile habitats like shallow seas. Large groups of insects and plants suffered only minor losses in past extinctions.

Complete fossil records for a number of marine invertebrate species show that marine invertebrate species survive from 1 to 10 million years. To compare extinction rates for an organism during different periods, extinction rates must be standardized. Scientists often express the extinction rate as the number of species that become extinct each million years that a species survives, or as extinctions per million species years (E/MSY). On this scale, the background rate for the marine invertebrates would range from a high of 1 E/MSY to a low of 0.1 E/MSY. Scientists have also calculated survival times for several terrestrial vertebrate species and come up with approximately 1 E/MSY for these species.

Current extinction rates for some organisms are more easily assessed than are background extinction rates, but scientists still only estimate; they don't know with certainty the number of species that currently exist. Only about 1.7 million species have been named, but by analyzing the rates at which new species are discovered and by estimating for groups such as bacteria that have been poorly studied, biologists believe that the number of species now present on earth is between 5 and 100 million. This means that most of the species that become extinct will do so without our ever knowing they existed. Even for a large and visible species, it is not easy to decide if the species has become extinct. How long after the last sighting do we wait before deciding it is gone forever? How hard do we look? If it is an endemic species — found only in a single place — we can be more certain, especially if it is a commonly recognized animal such as a bird. But if the organism has an extensive range and lives in many places, the pronouncement of extinction is more difficult. In addition, how do we decide whether two populations of organisms are the same or different species if they are similar but not morphologically identical? It's usually impossible to apply the standard definition of a species — the ability under natural conditions to produce viable, fertile offspring — and other criteria must be employed.

Even though it is difficult to compare ancient background extinction rates with recent extinction rates, because the criteria — fossil record versus human observation — are different, we present such comparisons here. They are crude indicators of what has happened, but they are sufficient to demonstrate a trend.

When scientists examine the extinction rate over the past 100 years for birds, mammals, reptiles, frogs, and freshwater clams, they find rates from 20 to 200 E/MSY. Extinction rates have jumped at least twentyfold; the high estimate for the current extinction episode is more than 1,000 times over the background level determined from the fossil record.

By looking at observational records of birds (about 9,000 species) and mammals (about 4,000 species), we discover that the rate of extinction has been accelerating over the past 400 years. According to these records, 38 species of birds and mammals became extinct from 1600 to 1810, in comparison with 112 species from 1810 to 1992. If we assume the average vertebrate species lasts for 1 million years, which the fossil record tells us, then we can compare the rate of extinction from the fossil record to those of the past 392 years. For simplicity, assume that evolution is linear, that 13,000 species of birds and mammals will become extinct and that no new species will evolve. We would then expect 0.013 species to go extinct each year, and at this rate, all birds and mammals now present would disappear in 1 million years. The actual rate of extinction has been 0.180 species per year from 1600 to 1810 and 0.651 per year from 1810 to 1992. Sadly, the rate of extinction rose about three and a half times from the first period to the second period, and in the second period the rate was an extraordinary 47 times the estimated prehuman rate, or 47 E/MSY. Hence, from 1810 to 1992, almost 1 percent of the earth's bird and mammal species checked out. At that rate all will be gone in 20,000 years — and much sooner than that if the rate continues to accelerate.

If we take into account the great reductions in biodiversity effected by human habitation, these estimates of current extinction rates are most likely too conservative. There are two reasons for this underestimation. First, when prehistoric humans entered a new habitat, they created disturbances that often led to a round of biodiversity loss and species extinctions — a pattern seen with other highly successful exotics: fire ants coming to the North American south, brown snakes to Guam, or common cats to New Zealand and Australia. Our best records of these human-caused disturbances and extinctions have been found on recently inhabited islands where we can look at places both before and after human habitation. Analyses of the Pacific islands show that prior to the initial human colonization by Polynesians, no birds had become extinct for thousands of years, but after the Polynesians arrived, more than 2,000 bird species became extinct. These 2,000 Pacific island species represent about 20 percent of the world's bird species, an example of human habitation touching off an extraordinarily large extinction.

Second, extinction is primarily driven by habitat fragmentation, degradation, or loss. Humans have converted close to 3.5 billion acres of ecosystems into crop land; reduced the world's forests by more than a third; dammed most rivers and filled in many swamps and estuaries in the northern hemisphere; and paved over, built on, mined, or otherwise rendered barren a sizable portion of the earth's ecologically productive land surface. These actions have radically diminished the area of many types of ecosystems; consequently, the size and number of habitats have been severely reduced. In the United States a historical analysis of ecosystem decline over the past several hundred years indicates that 30 ecosystems have been reduced by 98 percent or more, 58 by 85 percent or more, and 38 by 75 percent or more. These 126 ecosystems represent the majority of the significant ecosystems in the United States, including huge ecosystems like the tallgrass prairie east of the Missouri River, longleaf pine forests and savannas in the southeastern coastal plain, ungrazed sagebrush steppe in the Intermountain West, old-growth and other virgin stands in the eastern forest, and oak savanna in the Midwest. Also included are more restricted ecosystems such as alkali sink scrub in southern California, wet and mesic coastal prairies in Louisiana, and sedge meadows in Wisconsin.

These and similar worldwide habitat reductions have snuffed out many species, and the number of threatened species is growing. The 1996 IUCN Red List of Threatened Animals, published by the International Union for Conservation of Nature, lists over 5,000 species; 25 percent of all known mammal and 17 percent of all known bird species are on the threatened list. A 1996 Nature Conservancy study of more than 20,000 species native to the United States indicates that almost a third are rare or imperiled. Uncommon species often persist by migrating, but as human-kind continues on its path of ecosystem reduction, introduction of alien species, pollution, overharvesting, and occupying more space, these species will have fewer places to which to escape.

A critical difference in the current extinction episode is that significant numbers of plants have become extinct or are threatened with extinction. Over half the organisms known to have become extinct over the past 400 years are plants. The 1997 IUCN Red List of Threatened Plants indicates at least 12.5 percent of all known vascular plants — trees, shrubs, herbs, grasses, ferns — are threatened with extinction. The Nature Conservancy's 1996 study indicated that over 30 percent of the flowering plants in its survey are rare, imperiled, or believed extinct. These numbers are sobering because we know that plants are resilient, have simple needs, are the base of the food chain, and are the prime creators of habitat. Biodiversity decline has reached — or soon will reach — the numbers and rates associated with past episodes of mass extinction.

This sixth mass extinction is also unique because the cause — human beings — is not about to go away. Sixty-five million years ago when the asteroid jolted the planet, all hell broke loose, but then the healing began. This time biodiversity has been hammered relentlessly by human activities in ever more destructive ways: early on by simple overharvest-ing, primitive agriculture, moving a few species around, and impover-ishing a few local ecosystems; but now by our worldwide mixing of untold species, industrial farming, clear-cutting many of the earth's forests, overharvesting most of the oceans' fisheries, exposing the planet to ever-changing exotic chemicals with subtle as well as overwhelming toxicities, doubling nitrogen availability to ecosystems, and filling the earth's ecological space with more people and the residues of their habitation. In time, new selection pressure can elicit wondrous healing of extinction's losses, but continuously changing selection pressures merely impoverish without renewal.

Extinctions, even mass extinctions, are natural, so why should we be concerned? Many answers have been given; we consider three: First, the recovery time from a mass extinction event is measured in millions of years, and it takes 10 million or more years to return to the level of biodiversity that existed at the onset of the extinction episode. Since a vertebrate species survives for a million years on average, our species' chances of seeing even the early stages of recovery are slim. Second, the basis of future evolution is the diversity that exists now, so that the more severe the losses, the longer recovery will take. And the greater the losses, the greater the opportunities for new constellations of organisms, and hence, for species that persist after the extinction episode it will be more difficult to live through the onslaught of new life forms. If humans manage to survive the present extinction event, new diseases, new parasites, the competition from new species, and the chaotic state of renewal will present formidable challenges to our continued survival. The Permian extinction allowed dinosaurs to gain dominion over other land vertebrates, while the Cretaceous extinction removed the dinosaurs, thereby allowing mammals to evolve in the ecologically open landscape and to become the dominant land vertebrates. Third and most compelling because it relates directly to our current situation, human civilization utterly depends on existing biodiversity for its life-support functions. All mass extinctions have occurred in a radically altered world that experienced an extensive period of biological chaos, and it is highly unlikely that a civilization of billions of humans could weather such chaos.

The biodiversity that human civilization needs is not a subset of the earth's species found in a zoo or a botanical garden any more than the genes needed to make a human are a subset of the human genome in petri dishes. Species and genes survive and have biological meaning only in context; a species in a box or a DNA sequence in a test tube is in a vacuum — only in an ecosystem or in a cell does either become biologically relevant. Millions of years of evolution have honed biological relations in myriad ways that we don't understand now nor perhaps ever will. Assembling, species by species, an array of ecosystems that functions like the biosphere is as impossible as linking together isolated pieces of human DNA and producing a human being. We can take the biosphere and organisms apart, but we cannot re-create them.

Each ecosystem, like each species, is a result of its history. When a barren piece of land or a sterile aquatic environment is colonized by arriving species, it and the species begin to influence each other. Initial conditions — moisture level and range, temperature range, light quality and quantity, nutrient availability, physical character — are critical in dictating which species will successfully establish themselves. These colonizers modify conditions and create new habitats. Subsequent arrivals encounter conditions shaped by the colonization. Since the conditions and colonizers are always unique, the resulting ecosystem is a one-of-a-kind event. Nonetheless, we can categorize general ecosystems according to conditions, types of colonizers, and selection pressures.

All ecosystems perform functions like energy acquisition and flow, nutrient acquisition and cycling, and habitat creation. Which species do what, and how, varies. The same species in two ecosystems can perform functions of different value and in different degrees. For instance, when colonizing barren ground, lichens and mosses can play a major role in soil formation, nutrient enrichment, moisture retention, and habitat creation; in an established forest they may live on tree trunks and play no significant role in any of these functions. If only a few species constitute an ecosystem, each of these species can play a major role with little functional overlap. Suppose that only one plant species provides all the energy that flows through the ecosystem. If it is removed, the ecosystem will fall apart unless the vital function of energy acquisition is taken up by another photosynthetic species. If twenty species of plants are present in an ecosystem, those organisms all provide energy. Thus the ecosystem is far more resilient to perturbations and plant species loss than one with a single plant. The correlation between number of species and resiliency is unpredictable because some ecosystems, like bogs, function well with few species and others, like coral reefs, require many more species. Regardless of particular conditions, ecosystems are built of species in assemblages that perform ecosystem functions because of the unique relations among the constituent species.

When an ecosystem is first formed, after some disruption has impoverished the biodiversity of an area, the relations among species and ecosystem functions develop in an opportunistic fashion and usually operate ineffectively and inefficiently. Over time, as more species arrive, selection pressures and chance events produce competitive and cooperative interactions that lead to more effective and efficient relations. During this period some species are lost, while others coevolve unique associations. After hundreds, thousands, or sometimes millions of years, immensely intricate relations evolve to create a constellation of organisms that maintain ecosystem integrity while responding to normal environmental fluctuations. When viewed as a whole, the ecosystem may appear stable, but changes continually occur. Population sizes are not constant, sometimes varying a thousandfold or more, and species are routinely lost and gained. Species are rarely distributed uniformly but form a mosaic in constant change, like a kaleidoscope. In time, episodes of large-scale disturbance, such as glaciation, wipe the slate clean, and ecosystem creation begins anew.

These descriptions are accurate as general guidelines for understanding ecosystem creation and function, but they do not sufficiently describe a specific ecosystem, because each ecosystem is a unique, ongoing historic process subject only to the laws of nature. Western science has employed a reductionistic approach in seeking to identify universally applicable principles for making predictions. In biology, reductionism has been phenomenally successful at the cellular and molecular levels, because every cell, the fundamental unit of life, apparently shares a common ancestor or ancestors. As a result, all organisms have in common cellular and molecular features. At higher levels of organization — tissues, organs, organ systems, individuals, species — many lineages that arose during the evolution of multicellular organisms acquired features and systems that accomplish similar tasks but are not evolutionarily connected. For instance, the systems responsible for bringing oxygen to cells of insects, mammals, and flowering plants are different although they accomplish the same function. The principles of mammalian respiratory systems are of no value in predicting how oxygen is delivered to plant cells except at the level of chemistry and physics that describe, for example, the diffusion of oxygen across a cell membrane.

Ecosystems present us with a similar impedance to prediction, because ecological principles of ecosystem organization and function are explanatory but not predictive. They have limited value when we try to predict precisely an ecosystem's response to a disturbance, like Darwin and Wallace's powerful explanation of evolution by natural selection, which really can't predict outcomes. Although some scientists believe our inability to make accurate predictions in ecology resides in our limited knowledge, others contend that our failures in prediction are inevitable because each ecosystem is unique and because ecosystems are so complex, with so many interdependencies and regulative capacities, that outcomes are unknowable except in a general way. More knowledge will help us to understand ecosystems; however, it is presumptuous to believe that new knowledge will improve the accuracy of prediction in ecology beyond that of, say, meteorologists; nor will we manage the earth's ecosystems with any confidence about outcomes. Rather, in light of the consequences of our being wrong, we would be prudent to recognize our eternal ignorance and to act within a sphere compatible with maintaining healthy ecosystems.

As we push hard against the biodiversity that sustains us, we disturb ecosystems and throw them off balance. Despite our best intentions, when we attempt to aggressively manage complex, highly evolved ecosystems, our eternal ignorance guarantees failure. For example, at the turn of the century Flathead Lake in Montana supported a substantial population of cutthroat trout. To improve the fishing, kokanee salmon were stocked in 1916, but soon they displaced the prized cutthroat trout. In a few decades salmon by the thousands were migrating up McDonald Creek each autumn to spawn where grizzly bears, eagles, coyotes, gulls, and others came to depend on the fish and their eggs for food. For the migrating eagles these salmon replaced the bison carcasses that had recently disappeared from the plains and the Pacific salmon that, blocked by numerous dams, no longer reached the headwaters of the Columbia and Snake Rivers to spawn. In the 1960s, to increase the food supply for the kokanee salmon and thereby boost their population, state fisheries officials began stocking the upper portions of the streams that flowed into Flathead Lake with a non-native shrimp. But the shrimp spent the day at the bottom of the stream away from the surface-feeding salmon, and during the night they fed on the same zooplankton that the salmon ate during the day. The shrimp were not only unavailable to the young salmon for food, but they also ate the salmon's food. By the late 1980s, few salmon remained to spawn, and the eagles, grizzly bears, and others were again seeking another source of food.

The unintentional introductions of foreign species have also done untold damage to ecosystems. An entrepreneur brought the gypsy moth from Europe to Massachusetts late in the nineteenth century in hope of starting a silk industry. Some moths escaped from their cages and have been devouring northeastern forests ever since. Forty natural enemies of the gypsy moth have been introduced. Ten survived, but only one can control the invader. Even so, this imported control agent and about 90 native predators have yet to bring the moth into balance with the forests.

When species are eliminated through commercial exploitation, superficially similar ecosystems can be affected in different ways because of unappreciated variations. In the forests of Washington, Oregon, and California some clear-cuts will not grow trees despite several plantings, while neighboring clear-cuts support vigorous regrowth. The difference is in the soil microorganisms. After a clear-cut the populations of soil organisms — fungi, bacteria, nematodes, springtails, mites — are decimated as functional relations are destroyed. Log skidders and other heavy equipment disrupt and compact the soil, while brush-clearing fires change soil chemistry and sterilize the soil. Applied fumigants kill fungi and herbicides reduce competing vegetation, and both destroy relations among organisms. All rooted plants, including trees, have extensive associations with soil organisms that influence their growth. In some of these areas, the disruptions of clear-cutting were so great that the critical plant-microorganism associations could not be reestablished, and when the planted trees did not survive, the forest failed to regrow.

The environmental buildup of normally occurring substances that results from human activities may also damage forests, and other ecosystems, indirectly. Each year about 130 billion kilograms of nitrogen gas from the air are converted into ammonia and nitrate by natural processes and then circulate through the earth's ecosystems. Human activities now fix at least another 130 billion kilograms of nitrogen annually through producing fertilizer, burning fossil fuel, draining wetlands, burning forests, and planting nitrogen-fixing crops like peas, beans, and alfalfa. In many ecosystems nitrogen is a limiting nutrient. Adding nitrogen to the soil enables fast-growing plants to out-compete slow growers that are better adapted to nitrogen-limited conditions, which reduces plant diversity. Nitrates seep into streams and lakes, where they diminish water quality. Excess nitrates also mobilize alkaline elements like calcium and magnesium, and this makes soils more susceptible to acidification by acid rain, caused partly by nitrous oxide, which occurs as a result of burning fossil fuels. Plant scientists also suspect that excess nitrogen in the soil weakens relations between mycorrhizal fungi and tree roots. Under normal circumstances the tight symbiotic relation between roots and mycorrhizae prevents other organisms from infecting the roots and causing disease. With the root-mycorrhizal association weakened, pathogens invade. As more trees sicken and die, less nitrogen is taken up (that is, more remains in the soil) and forest decline increases. This scenario may explain the damage in many European forests over the past fifty years.

These examples and thousands more demonstrate two simple truths: our capability to disrupt and reduce biodiversity is strong, yet our capacity to manage it is weak. If we wish to perpetuate our global civilization as we push hard against the biodiversity that sustains us, accepting and acting on these two truths are imperative. This understanding prompts a most profound question: how much and what kinds of biodiversity do current human civilizations require to create sustainable cultures? Only when we have destroyed too much will it be possible to know something essential to human existence has become extinct. Even if we figure it out, by then it will be too late.

Rapa Nui provides a simple and instructive example of the dependent relations between a civilization and its biodiversity. The biodiversity on Rapa Nui allowed for a people that produced huge stone statues, hunted birds on land and porpoises at sea, grew crop plants, and maintained a population of thousands. Their population peak, as we know, was reached perhaps two hundred years after the peak of statue building when porpoise hunting was no longer possible and the birds and forests had been driven to extinction. As the forests, birds, and sea provided less and then no food, agricultural technology substituted for the lost resources and brought more food to the growing population. During this shift, which took several hundred years, the culture and the impoverished biological resource base interacted to maintain each other, but over time they became insupportable. The population along with the culture collapsed when technology could no longer substitute for the lost physical and biological resources. The demise of the Rapa Nui shows that in culture-biodiversity relationships, danger signals may only appear long after the actions that generated them. Often the signals come too late to salvage the resource base. Looking back on the Rapa Nui, we see clearly that when the palm and the forests became extinct, the traditional culture was doomed, although it continued, propped by more intensive agriculture, for hundreds of years after.

How many palm trees and other species did the Rapa Nui need to sustain their civilization? How much biodiversity would have been sufficient for the forests to absorb all of the normal environmental fluctuations and still remain intact? These are not simple questions, and we face the same questions on a global scale. As we attempt to determine biodiversity requirements, our errors in analysis and policy are difficult to identify and correct, and the consequences are impossible to predict. This sobering reality is heightened by the fact that Earth may now be like Rapa Nui in about 1000 C.E. Primary forests are in steep decline, countless bird species have become extinct and many more are endangered, marine resources are seriously overexploited, human population has far exceeded ecological norms, and our ability to destroy life continues to expand.

What makes our situation even more dire than that of the Rapa Nui is that they, like all prehistoric peoples, primarily disrupted only the upper part of the ecological pyramid: birds, fish, trees, and so on. Modern civilization is disrupting not only what remains at the top but the entire pyramid, including its base: plants, fungi, insects, bacteria, and all other organisms that act in concert to flow energy and cycle nutrients. Our industrial economy is wreaking havoc upon the atmosphere and upon every ecosystem on the planet by introducing novel synthetic compounds and natural compounds in excessive concentrations. Both types of chemical pollution disrupt ecosystems at all levels.

Synthesized chlorofluorocarbons now in the upper atmosphere are breaking down into reactive molecules that catalyze the destruction of stratospheric ozone and increase life-threatening ultraviolet B (UV-B) radiation at the earth's surface. Some crop plants, marine phytoplankton, amphibians, and a host of other organisms, are suffering as a result of their sensitivity to higher levels of UV-B radiation. Although added UV-B radiation will certainly cause an increase in the number of human cancers, far more serious consequences will arise from disruptions in agricultural and other ecosystems. The emergence in the late 1980s of global agreements to phase out chlorofluorocarbons is a positive event that may allow the ozone layer to recover sometime late in the next century, if we are lucky.

The substantial increase of greenhouse gases in the atmosphere, a result of human activities, is far more problematic than the destruction of the ozone, however. The atmosphere is relatively transparent to the sun's light but absorbs the infrared radiation that Earth radiates back toward space. The topsides of clouds reflect sunlight back into space but absorb about 20 percent of the infrared radiation that strikes them. Water vapor, carbon dioxide, nitrous oxide, methane, and other trace gases also retain infrared radiation and thereby keep the planet warm. Without these influences, the earth's surface temperature would be much cooler, perhaps as much as 33°C. Over the last 100 years the earth's surface has warmed about 0.5°C; human-caused increases in greenhouse gases have been the determining factor in this global warming. Carbon dioxide from burning fossil fuels and deforestation appears a major cause of this increase, although other gases associated with human activities have also contributed to this effect.

Current growth trends in economic activity and population indicate future levels of greenhouse gases in the atmosphere will be substantially higher than today; these, in turn, are projected to raise the earth's average temperature 1–5°C over the next century. While these changes may seem trivial to readers accustomed to fantastic growth rates in production or standards of living, we must bear in mind that the biosphere operates in a narrow range of "wellness," just as many organisms perish if their habitat temperature changes by even a few degrees. Furthermore, this rate of change is 10 to 50 times more rapid than the average increase of 1°C per 1,000 years that occurred between the end of recent glacial periods and the warm interglacial times. This historically rapid climate change will put extreme stress on ecosystems and civilization alike. Ecosystems may change unpredictably, and although the impact may be reduced by migration or moving organisms from one ecosystem to another, many organisms won't relocate fast enough to stay within their climate range.

For a long time we have known that our activities exact a toll on the biodiversity that supports our civilizations. More than 2,000 years ago Plato recognized that cutting down forests resulted in soil erosion and dried-up springs. Historical and archeological records depict the collapse of cultures through environmental degradation and the loss of biodiversity. Although Western peoples have failed historically to validate patterns of living that have valued and preserved biodiversity, contemporary scientific explanations of physical and biological reality now give us insights into our relations with the rest of life. Industrialized societies now know that they are a part of an amazing biological enterprise and thus subject to the natural laws imposed on all life.

Even though we may appreciate the importance of preserving biodiversity, even biologists do not know how much biodiversity will sustain civilization or for how long. Since most ecosystems and habitats have been devastated and so many species have become extinct in the last few hundred years, we might wish to save everything that is left; however, this is impossible. As a result of our past actions, tens of thousands of organisms are already on the brink of extinction and many are beyond rescue. A large fraction of earth's ecosystems has been eliminated, simplified, and radically altered. Until the entire world — all of its nations and diverse peoples — responds aggressively to the biodiversity crisis as the top priority issue, development and the emphasis on economic growth will continue to drive even more species and ecosystems to extinction. We may not be able to save everything, but the more we lose the more limited our options will be.

Chapter Seven

The Market:
Master or Servant?

Only economists still put the cart before the horse by claiming that the growing turmoil of mankind can be eliminated if prices are right. The truth is that only if our values are right will prices also be so.

NICHOLAS GEORGESCU-ROEGEN, *Energy and Economic Myths*

The human economy cannot be reduced to a natural system. There is more to the idea of value than embodied energy or survival advantage. But neither can the economy subsume the entire natural system under its managerial dominion of efficient allocation. This vision of the earth as an alchemist's centrally planned terrarium, with nothing wild or spontaneous but everything base transformed into gold, into its highest instrumental value for humans, is a sure recipe for disaster.

HERMAN DALY, *Beyond Growth*

AMONG THE INDIANS of eastern Canada a craving for material objects is considered a disease. The treatment involves isolating the individual and lavishing the patient with gifts until he or she is cured. In western North America, groups of coastal Indians in British Columbia accord honor and prestige to those who give away their possessions in a special ceremony, the potlatch, which is an earned privilege. Accounts of these and numerous other cultures offer glimpses of human behavior far different from that guided by market relations and Western ideas of individualism. Our present socially constructed industrial economy may encourage consumption and in general discourage sustainable lifestyles; however, for most of human existence, throughout the world, these patterns did not exist. It is impossible, therefore, to conclude that market economies are "natural."

The dominance of individual-based, impersonal exchange — central to modern markets — is a recent human invention, as is the concept of money as a universal means of valuing all goods and services by the same standard. Within the last century Western civilization has honed the concept of money-based market exchange so that it cuts deeply into earth's cultural fabric. The concept is so pervasive that most people in industrialized cultures equate value with money, but this is a learned, culturally derived attitude — people have to be taught it. World capitalism and its market economy are not merely a way of organizing resources but also a manifestation of a powerful system of cultural beliefs. Attitudes toward nature, human relations, and power are all essential components of the market economy.

On the timescale of a human life, Nauru's transition to a money-based, market economy was slow. Traditionally, Nauruans did not need money because they had their own means of allocating resources so that all could satisfy their needs and wants. Material objects — land, birds, or fish — had value; and use rights existed for coconut trees, designs, and songs. Material things and rights changed owners in the context of cultural traditions, not by means of some universal equivalent like money. The concept on which a money-based, market economy rests was foreign to Nauruans. How could the life-sustaining functions of a coconut tree be equated with inert coins and paper? Why did they need to save money for the future when tomorrow had always taken care of itself? Above all, the Nauruans' cultural heritage had been maintained by distancing themselves from foreigners and by embracing the traditionally close ties with family and clan. Only as interactions with and dependence on the outside world became unavoidable did the integration of a market economy into Nauruan society slowly take place.

In the early contacts between Nauruans and Europeans, barter enabled Europeans to acquire pigs, fish, coconuts, and copra from the Nauruans. With barter, manufactured goods and foods were introduced gradually, except for guns, which rapidly became popular commodities. Items like canned fish were oddities at first and took decades to become common in the Nauruan diet. Although trading was established in the nineteenth century, most Western products remained unimportant in native life. The initiation of phosphate mining brought opportunities for economic gain by working, but the Nauruans did not care to participate, for they did not need money and saw no reason to acquire it, leaving hundreds of foreigners to dig, haul, load, and take away the phosphate. Early in the twentieth century, the Nauruans laughed at the white man who fished when he was not hungry. But soon, some Nauruans were fishing to sell their catch to foreigners on their island. The small sums that came from phosphate royalty payments and from the sale of copra and fish provided the cash Nauruans used for the few Western extras they purchased.

Even after the concept of a money economy was introduced to Nauruans, strong family bonds and cultural identity nurtured their traditional patterns. Although the beachcombers had been Western civilization's first emissaries, in the early twentieth century it was the missionaries, not phosphate mining, who most seriously devalued Nauruan culture. Christian missionaries pushed hard to eradicate traditional patterns of dress and behavior such as those related to dancing, singing, sexuality, and marriage. With regard to material objects, they were persuaded to believe that the old crafts and ways of living were inferior and to prefer woven cloth and china plates to pandanus-leaf *ridis* and coconut-shell utensils. Despite the assaults on their economy, few joined the workforce: in 1933 fewer than 50 in an adult male population of over

500 worked for money. Thus, even into the 1930s the Nauruans were distinct from the intruders who were hollowing out their island — not just in how they lived but also in what they valued.

Although they had not joined the workforce, they certainly realized that they were not getting their fair share of the money from the sale of phosphate. In 1921 the British Phosphate Commissioners raised the rate they paid to landowners from one-half pence (1 pound sterling = 20 shillings = 240 pence) per ton of phosphate mined to one and a half pence. By 1924, when phosphate sold for just under two and a half pounds per ton, the Nauruans pressed for one shilling per ton with one and a half pence to be held in trust for all Nauruans and three pounds annual rent for each acre whether being mined or not. The commissioners gave the Nauruans a new agreement in 1927 of seven and a half pence per ton mined and a one-time payment of 40 pounds per acre mined. The commissioners believed they were more than generous, but the Nauruans understood just how little they were being given. The Nauruans did not aggressively seek a larger share because they believed the supply of phosphate would last several hundred years and hence give them plenty of time to improve the deal. By 1939 they were receiving directly or indirectly about 9 percent of the phosphate revenues; even this percentage is not as generous as it seems, because the sale price of Nauruan phosphate was less than half of the prevailing world market price.

The Western economic presence had deleterious effects on the health of the Nauruans. Phosphate mining brought a huge influx of foreigners who carried diseases that devastated the Nauruan population — 150 deaths in 1907 from dysentery, 50 in 1910 from infantile paralysis, and 100 in 1920 from influenza. In 1925, with a total Nauruan population of 1,220, 189 were isolated with leprosy, and another 365 were being treated for the disease. In 1927, 10 people had tuberculosis and another 4 died from the disease. In the mid 1920s the infant death rate was over 300 per 1,000 live births. These high infant-mortality rates were eventually traced to a vitamin B1 deficiency due to changed eating habits. Too little toddy, the major natural source of vitamin B1 on the island, was being drunk; and many infants were no longer breast-fed. The islanders now depended on Western medicine for survival, a factor that contributed to their need to participate in the market economy.

As diseases were brought under control, the population grew. When the Japanese invaded on August 26, 1942, the Nauruan population exceeded 1,800, yet their island and their lives were again radically changed. The Japanese not only wanted the phosphate, they also valued Nauru's strategic location in the Pacific. The Japanese placed barbed-wire entanglements and dug deep ditches in the reef as defenses against invasion. The entire 20-kilometer circumference was fortified with two rings of machine gun bunkers, as well as large-caliber gun emplacements. After an airfield was completed by the occupiers in January 1943, Nauru was bombed regularly until the Japanese capitulated in August 1945.

Soon after the start of the war almost 7,000 people populated Nauru: 3,000 Japanese military personnel, 1,500 Korean laborers, several hundred detainees from Banaba, about 200 Chinese phosphate workers, and just under 2,000 Nauruans. The several Europeans who had remained to look after the phosphate works were terminated by the Japanese after the first major Allied bombing of the airfield destroyed Japanese planes on the ground. In the summer of 1943, over 1,200 Nauruans were deported to Truk in the Caroline Islands, and the 49 lepers from the leper station were taken out to sea and drowned. Of the 600 or so Nauruans remaining on the island, about 90 died during the occupation. On Truk another 463 died before the survivors were returned to Nauru in January 1946.

The war had profoundly affected the people of Nauru, whose prospects for the future were now radically compromised. One out of every 3 had died; the young and old were the most severely victimized. The island itself was a battle-scarred remnant of its former self. The condition of the Nauruans and their island made them even more dependent on and vulnerable to the market economy.

Before the war a Nauruan could live well without becoming a for-pay laborer in the market economy. After the war, there was no choice but to work for pay. Countless coconut trees had been uprooted or otherwise damaged, homes and villages had been razed, and the fabric of Nauruan social life had been torn almost beyond repair. No phosphate had been mined since early 1942, and thus no royalties had been paid. During the war the Nauruans' captors had forced their prisoners to work, but now the need for money and the opportunity for work combined to move Nauruans into the workforce. In 1948, 88 percent of the males over 16 years of age were employed by the British Phosphate Commissioners, the Administration of the island, or the Nauru Co-operative Store.

The General Assembly of the United Nations made Nauru a trust territory under the protection of the Trusteeship Council; Australia was the administering authority acting on behalf of Great Britain, New Zealand, and itself. As with the League of Nations' mandate, by accepting the trusteeship of Nauru, Australia, the de facto administrator, again accepted as "a sacred trust" the task of making Nauru independent and self-governing. In 1948 Nauruans made their first formal request to the Trusteeship Council for a voice in administration policies and some control of their island's finances. The Australians convinced the Nauruan Council of Chiefs to withdraw the request, which began years of stonewalling by Australians and the British Phosphate Commissioners to prevent Nauruans from gaining independence and control of the phosphate industry.

In this arrangement, too, the West's cultural myths are manifest. Australians and other westerners associated their management of Nauru's phosphate industry with the progress of humanity; they maintained that through the generosity of the Administration and the British Phosphate Commissioners, the Nauruans were cared for well. In this paternalistic view the Nauruans were not able to manage their own affairs, nor could they be educated or trained to govern Nauru and to run the phosphate industry. The ecological integrity of Nauru and the will of its people were easily overlooked in the West's promotion of the greater good of world economic growth. Thousands of policies and actions by the Australians and the British Phosphate Commissioners affirmed and perpetuated these beliefs. For example, the policy of not recruiting trained teachers made the Nauruan educational system inadequate in preparing students for study abroad; and their failure to become educated reinforced the Western bias that Nauruans were backward and suitable for only low-level jobs. Paternalism and racism, then, slowed the move to self-government and isolated the Nauruans.

The broader worldview was changing, however. White-male superiority was being challenged from many sides. The United Nations' Trusteeship Council raised many objections to the slow progress toward independence on Nauru, but for years the objections were deflected, often because the Australians and the British Phosphate Commissioners were unwilling to provide hard data on the finances of the phosphate mining industry on Nauru. It was to the Australians' advantage to maintain the status quo because Australian farmers bought phosphate at less than half the world-market price. Through the 1950s two main issues came to dominate the debates concerning Nauru. The first concerned the phosphate industry: royalty payments and ownership. The second was Nauru's fate and that of its people. Would the island be habitable when the phosphate was gone? Could the mined-out areas be rehabilitated? Would the Nauruans be resettled somewhere else? Would they remain together as an independent group?

Under the leadership of Hammer DeRoburt, a schoolteacher who was elected to the Local Government Council and became head chief in 1956, the Nauruans emerged as competent and uncompromising negotiators. For more than a decade the Australians and the British Phosphate Commissioners kept the United Nations' Trusteeship Council at bay, but the tenacity and shrewdness of the Nauruan negotiators eventually won out. After eighty years of foreign control, on January 31, 1968, the Nauruans regained control of their home and became the smallest independent nation in the world.

They were not the same people, though, nor was it the same island that the *Hunter*'s crew first observed in 1798. At least one-third of Topside was mined-out coral pinnacles. Over 6,000 people lived on the island, more than half of them foreigners. Many Nauruans now traced their lineages to African and European beachcombers and more recently to Marshall and Caroline Islanders, Gilbert and Ellice Islanders, and Banabans. Most men worked for money. The functioning of their island and their lives totally depended on the outside world and its money-based market economy, yet what kind of culture did they have? It was not Western, nor was it Nauruan. The myths that now informed who they were and how they should live were muddled and contradictory.

In 1968, Nauruans were faced with difficult choices. In view of the devastation of their island and culture, what would be the best course of action? Should they close down the phosphate industry, expel all foreigners, and draw up a long-term plan to restore the island's biodiversity and to curb their own population so it could be sustained by Nauru's resources? Or should they let the market dictate the outcome: continue to mine the phosphate until it is gone, use the money to participate in the world economy, import whatever they can afford, and let their population continue to grow with the resources purchased from the outside?

Nauruans chose the latter path — or at least they took the latter path — because, one might argue, they did not imagine that such a choice existed. Now, over thirty years later, they have almost exhausted the phosphate. Income from mining profits saved in trust funds is intended to provide for their needs now that the original source of these profits, phosphate, will soon be gone.

Since at least the time of Adam Smith two hundred years ago, progress has been equated with the growth and expansion of economic activity, fueled by massive increases in energy use and in materials flowing through human economies. The term "gross domestic product," or GDP — the total market-based transactions within the borders of a country in a particular year — came into use in the second quarter of the twentieth century as a measure of market-based transactions. Despite its many shortcomings, GDP is the economic indicator most often used to assess economic health and progress. For instance, GDP does not measure nonmarket activity such as work done in the home or transactions of barter exchange, nor does it distinguish between interrelated, nonproductive activities — money spent hauling toxic wastes to a dump site and money spent cleaning up the waste site if the toxins leak into the surrounding area and become a health hazard. Nor does GDP adequately take into account human well-being or the condition of the biological environment in which the economic activity takes place. Nevertheless, a primary goal of politicians everywhere is to sustain GDP growth. In this economic context, well-being, at least for most of the planet's inhabitants, is assumed positively and directly linked to market activity and only remotely connected to the environmental base that ultimately makes economic activity possible.

Nauru illustrates the problem associated with the blanket assumption that improving human well-being and maintaining environmental health are positively correlated with increasing GDP. The island's GDP has risen phenomenally since the turn of the century, yet the natural environment, the health of the Nauruans, and their traditional culture have been severely degraded and impoverished over the same period.

Examples like Nauru have stimulated some economists over the last several decades to seriously rethink the relations among natural resources, human and societal health, and economic activity. Now many question what the economist Joseph Schumpeter called the "pre-analytic" assumptions of neoclassical economics. Among these assumptions are that more is always preferable to less, that everything has a substitute, and, most important, that the natural world is, for all practical purposes, a subset of the human economy. Even now, most economists still hold that the natural world has value only if it contributes to economic well-being measured in monetary terms. Other economists argue that the assumptions of neoclassical theory, and the rules of the market system described by the theory, conflict with the long-term health of physical and biological systems. These contrarian economists are beginning to question the beliefs that unlimited material growth is possible, or even desirable, and that substitutes can always be found for the functions of the physical and biological worlds.

Phosphate mining on Nauru illustrates what economists call "weak sustainability," a concept relevant to the debate over sustainable development now engaging economists, biologists, environmentalists, and policy makers. Weak sustainability is based on a simple but astute rule of investment: Do not sustain today's consumption by using up your capital. GDP may be seen as the return on capital investment, so an economy is weakly sustainable if total capital is not decreasing. "Capital" is anything used in the production of other goods, including manufactured capital like machines and factories, financial capital, and "natural capital," the features of the natural world used to produce economic goods. A fundamental assumption of modern economics is fungibility; that is, economic goods have substitutes. Thus, natural and other kinds of capital are assumed substitutes; natural capital may be decreased so long as there is a compensating increase in other kinds of capital. Under weak sustainability, it is permissible to destroy part of the environment if its economic value as capital is transformed into another kind of capital. We can chop down a rain forest and sell the wood if a dollar amount equivalent to the forest's lost capacity to produce economic goods is invested in something else — a chain saw factory, for instance.

Weak sustainability is not only an abstract economic concept but also an accurate description of how markets operate. In market economies the value of all resources used for production and of all consumer goods bought and sold is measured by a single standard: money. Everything is a commodity and every commodity has its price, and if the price is high enough it will be sold — traded for money. The market system is a powerful and efficient mechanism for finding and generating substitutes for resources as they become scarce. Because the value of manufactured capital and natural resources can be measured by the single standard of money, they are potential substitutes in the market. Weak sustainability follows the logic of the market, which assumes perfect substitutability between natural resources and manufactured capital.

Nauru's economy is sustainable according to the assumptions underlying the concept of weak sustainability. The trust funds owned by the Nauruans are estimated to exceed $1 billion, which have the capacity to yield an enormous amount of interest income. So long as the Nauruan trust funds are large enough and continue to grow fast enough, future generations will be provided for and will live well materially. Poor investments — the Nauruans have made many — or severe economic disruptions, like those in Asia in the late 1990s, could lead to big losses that might make their financial situation more tenuous.

At the planetary level, weak sustainability is a recipe for disaster. The materials and functions of biodiversity are absolutely necessary for our well-being, and although substitutability between natural resources and functions and human-produced capital and services may be permissible sometimes, at other times it is impossible. A highway and trucks can substitute for a river when transporting logs, but for other environmental features substitution may not be possible. For example, we know of no substitute for an atmosphere whose proper mix of gases permits temperatures compatible with life.

Weak sustainability is correlated to our ability to substitute human-produced services for nature's functions; however, manufactured economic capacity cannot replace many such functions. It is also highly uncertain whether these functions — pollination, soil formation, genetic resources, climate regulation, and others — could ever be replaced by human technologies on a planetary scale even if the monetary, material, and human resources could be mustered. In addition, the substitution is usually irreversible — money cannot bring back extinct species or restore radically impoverished ecosystems.

As the case of Nauru shows, however, replacing formerly "free" functions of nature with manufactured services can raise GDP. For example, replacing the water purification services of a wetland with a sewage treatment plant may improve the economy by creating jobs and income where none existed before. In economies able to mobilize capital quickly, if the destruction of the wetland leads to flooding and property damage, the resulting construction jobs and additional income increase the GDP. The adverse effects of destroying wetlands — losing habitat, losing genetic resources, and adding greenhouse gases that accelerate global climate change — will happen so far in the future that the costs of these effects are counted as negligible. Thus, weak sustainability as a policy for guaranteeing the well-being of future generations is problematic.

"Strong sustainability," an alternative resource policy suggested by ecological economists, distinguishes between renewable resources — fisheries, forests, potable water, and so on — and nonrenewable resources — minerals, fossil fuels, and others — and sets limits on resource use by scaling market activity to the biosphere. Strong sustainability has three rules: use renewable resources at rates of harvest below the natural rate of regeneration, keep waste flows below the assimilative capacity of the affected systems, and extract nonrenewable resources at a rate less than or equal to the rate substitutes are found. For example, we can harvest salmon from a stream at a rate that does not reduce the quantity and quality of returning salmon. We can also discharge wastes into the stream and the ocean at rates that will not disrupt the functioning of the stream or ocean with regard to salmon production. Nonrenewable resources may be used, but their stocks must be maintained by increases in proven reserves, recycling, and efficiency of use, or the discovery of substitutes. Thus, in principle, future generations have the same or equivalent resources as did past generations. Strong sustainability denies that natural resources and manufactured capital are substitutes and advocates the notion that nature is our endowment and that we should live off the interest of natural resources, not the principal.

The recognition that human activities must be scaled to nature's capacities is a major advance in economic thinking. Even so, our understanding of markets, ecosystems, and population dynamics is rudimentary. As a consequence, scaling our activities to nature's capacities is a big challenge, one that also makes strong sustainability problematic as an operational concept or as a policy guide. Determining the sustainable level for harvesting fish is a case in point. Fish populations have natural fluctuations over decades-long periods that depend on climate cycles, the populations of other species, and other little understood factors. Human interventions only add to the impossibility of collecting data within a period relevant to establishing catch quotas. The enforcement of the regulatory concept of maximum sustainable yield has failed miserably because, inevitably, quotas have been too high and fish populations have fluctuated unpredictably. It has been politically impossible to manage fishing efforts and technologies to obtain sustainable harvests, and therefore most of the world's major fisheries are in decline or have collapsed. To change this, we must rely on knowledge of ecosystems so we can tailor our behavior to ecosystem functions rather than try to control biological resources. We have little hope of managing complex ecosystems, but we may be able to manage our behavior in relation to such ecosystems.

Strong sustainability also differs from weak sustainability in another fundamental way: it does not accept the assumption that economic well-being covers all concerns. Harmonious social relations within and between cultures, social justice, and equity are elements of human well-being that are poorly addressed, if at all, by market economies. Clearly, we must step outside the conventional market framework in order to establish the conditions for maintaining human well-being.

Competitive markets have proven an effective way to allocate resources. The material diversity and richness in the lives of many people in industrialized nations mainly derive from the power of these markets to mobilize resources for humans. When it comes to ensuring that the economy is enduring, though, the market system has serious shortcomings, which are apparent in the use and misuse of biodiversity. Much of the problem arises because ecosystems and markets operate on vastly different timescales. Ecosystems stabilize over periods measured in hundreds to thousands of years, a timescale well outside an individual's lifetime or a culture's duration. But market exchange and economic activity are driven by decisions made during a time period related to a human life span. This mismatch of timescales pits economic activity against ecological activity, because markets, by design, focus on the present and are blind to long-term environmental consequences and future human needs.

Ecosystems have myriad checks and balances and many hierarchical levels of interacting influences. While market systems are also hierarchical and complex, resource use is dictated by the single criterion of relative price. The price of a good or a productive input is assumed by most economists to contain the information necessary to make correct choices about resource use. Economic policy for environmental issues is, for most economists, one of getting the price right so it reflects the "true" value of environmental goods. In seeking to establish the appropriate price, economists have tried to go beyond market values and calculate use values (e.g., direct use of a river or of the atmosphere), option values (e.g., preserving a view or a forest for possible future use), and existence values (e.g., maintaining wilderness or a noneconomic species even if it is never used). At the same time most economists still assume that a single price, with the proper adjustments, can be an objective measure of the true value of an environmental good.

Although adjusting prices to reflect environmental costs and assigning property rights where none exist can certainly facilitate more rational use of biological resources, the main problem with price-based markets remains: it is impossible to assign a correct price to an environmental good such as the existence of a species or a function performed by an ecosystem. Since we have not identified most species — much less the interactions among them or the functions performed by the biosphere — it is dangerous and misleading to believe that a correct price can be assigned to them. What is the dollar value of the microclimate created by a forest? Or the steady flow of a river? Or the purification of water by a swamp? Or the sight of a soaring hawk? Or the production of oxygen by marine phytoplankton? Or the fungi in forest soil? If we could choose otherwise, would we continue to trust the market's ability to price biodiversity and other environmental features correctly and thereby decide the future of species and civilization? So far the market has set a zero price on preserving most biodiversity, which is why we are causing the earth's sixth mass extinction in the past 600 million years.

Market decisions are made by individuals at particular times. In industrialized and other cultures, impatience and uncertainty about the future create powerful motives to use resources now rather than at some later date. Individuals naturally discount the future. As a consequence, we are willing to pay a specific price for an item today but a lower price for having the item delivered at a later time. For instance, if you are willing to pay a dollar for a soda today, how much are you willing to pay today for a soda that will be delivered in five years? Certainly less than a dollar because you might not be alive in five years, because you could invest the dollar to earn interest between now and then, and because immediate gratification is more desirable than delayed gratification. For the biosphere, discounting the future encourages current generations to destroy irreplaceable biological resources regardless of the biological and social consequences for future generations. Thus, if you invested in an old-growth forest for its trees and they were growing at 1 percent per year while the interest rate was 6 percent per year, it would make economic sense to cut the trees and convert them into money because you would earn 6 percent instead of 1 percent on your investment. The analysis is more complex than this example, but in our current market context such assessment is blind to biological features and to the needs of future generations.

Market systems use relative prices to allocate resources in production and consumption. A necessary condition for an efficiently operating market is that producers and consumers be fully informed of the characteristics of goods and productive inputs. Reliable information about the productivity of inputs and the utility, or satisfaction, derived from products consumed is critical if participants in the market economy are to put appropriate prices on market goods. Markets allocate scarce goods and services in a way that everyone achieves maximum utility within her or his income constraints based on initial income distribution. With biological resources, though, we are uninformed about characteristics, and we lack ways to assess the value of many aspects of biodiversity; hence, it is impossible for markets to allocate biological resources so as to guarantee ecosystem functions and productivity.

Economists generally believe that markets respond to scarcity by stimulating production of substitutes through price changes. In theory, plentiful items are priced lower than rare items that serve similar functions. If the price rises enough, economic incentives will propel the market to bring forth substitutes. All of us have seen many of these substitutions among metals, plastics, glass, energy sources, and so on over the years as supply, demand, and efficiencies interplay to create products at competitive prices. The market has succeeded in preventing shortages of most raw materials. When markets do not work efficiently, economists look for the explanation in places external to the market: governmental policies, monopolistic controls, or failure to assign property rights. Many successes in market function — as well as establishing the causes of market failures — have built economists' confidence in the market's ability to allocate biological resources in a sustainable fashion. However, the effects of market economies on biodiversity indicate that many biological resources are different from resources like iron, glass, oil, or phosphate.

Human use of animals highlights this difference and demonstrates a conflict between market activity and species preservation. In Asia an Indian rhinoceros horn when ground into powder and sold as an aphrodisiac is valued at around $100,000. Black bear gallbladders sell for $10,000 a kilogram in Japan, while a Siberian tiger is worth $25,000 in the Pacific Coast region of Russia. A single western Atlantic bluefin tuna recently sold for $83,500 in the Japanese sushi market. The phenomenally high market prices of these and other species have not called forth substitutes — there are no close substitutes — rather, the prices have encouraged hunting that will probably lead to extinction. Two case studies, one old and one new, illustrate why markets are a threat to maintaining biodiversity.

About 5 billion passenger pigeons were present in the Americas when

Europeans arrived. With the construction of railroads and the invention of refrigerated railroad cars in the second half of the nineteenth century, pigeons could be killed in the Midwest and shipped to the East Coast for consumption. In the 1860s, 7,500,000 pigeons were shipped from one county in Michigan in one year, while over 235,000 birds were shipped in a single day from Grand Rapids. The decimation that took place in the 1860s and 1870s predisposed the bird to extinction (the species was gone from the wild by 1900 and the last bird died in captivity in 1914), but market price did not signal the demise of the species: price per dozen birds from Milwaukee ranged from $0.40 to $0.85 in 1871 and from $0.75 to $1.00 in 1882, and in intervening years prices fell within the same range. We have substituted other animals for passenger pigeons as a food source, but we can never know the biological consequences of this extinction.

Atlantic bluefin tuna come in two stocks, western and eastern. The eastern stock is about twenty times as large as the western, and tagging experiments indicate minimal mixing of the two. Since they breed at different times, in different places, and under different water conditions, basic biology indicates that the two groups are already, or are at least becoming, reproductively isolated. Fish from the western stock command a higher market price than those from the eastern, because of the meat's taste and fat content, which are especially desirable in the Japanese sushi market. Since the most conservative economic analysis is based on zero mixing, we assume this in our analysis.

In the early 1970s two events, one social and the other technological, made the commercial bluefin tuna industry feasible. The Japanese sushi market expanded as the Japanese economy boomed in the 1960s and 1970s, and the development of air freight allowed fresh tuna to be shipped overnight to Japan. The inflation-adjusted price paid for western Atlantic bluefin tuna by Japanese importers jumped from $.05 per pound to $1 in 1973 and subsequently to $12 in 1986 and then more than $80 in 1994. The price received by fishermen went from $.20 per pound in 1973 to $14.00 in 1992 — a nineteenfold increase when adjusted for inflation. This price meant that, although the western Atlantic bluefin population declined 83 percent from a breeding stock of 70,000 metric tons in 1970 to 12,000 metric tons in 1992, the Consumer Price Index—adjusted monetary value of the stock increased threefold. Thus, a major biological decline shows up as a gain when measured in economic terms. Such discrepancies in valuation guarantee that current market systems are unable to preserve biodiversity.

Market outcomes are driven by millions of decisions made by producers and consumers. The environmental impact of each decision taken by itself is almost always negligible. A person's decision to eat, or not to eat, a hamburger made from beef grown on land that was formerly rain forest has no measurable impact on the destruction of rain forests to make room for cattle ranches, but the collective impact is huge. The market has no mechanism for addressing the unintended consequence of rain forest destruction because no short-term, negative feedback to individuals from the economic system can bring about corrective behavior. Incremental environmental damage does create negative feedback because the economic activity ceases when the ecosystem becomes dysfunctional or the population of the exploited species collapses. For example, the Hudson River no longer has a significant fishery, nor are the marginal lands of the southwestern United States used much for farming or cattle grazing; these ecosystems could not tolerate the imposed level and kind of human activity and still maintain the biological processes that made them economically productive in the first place.

Myriad other examples establish that the price-based market economy that dominates the planet is changing the entire environmental matrix. Erosion and loss of soil fertility; changes in the global geochemical cycles of nitrogen, carbon, and water; local and global changes in atmospheric composition and the resultant climate change; and the massive alterations of every ecosystem on the planet — all are for the most part the products of the immense global market economy. All are interconnected and gradually or dramatically diminish biodiversity, which disrupts the function and flow of materials from ecosystems crucial to the stability of civilized society. If we do not preserve the biodiversity that remains, we jeopardize world civilization. Clearly our global economic myths are moving earth's civilizations at a rapid pace into unknown and dangerous waters. This trajectory into merciless and uncharted seas, although unique in detail and by its global scale, has been experienced by earlier human cultures. Most have foundered but not all.

As Stephen Jay Gould once remarked, "Nature does not exist for us, had no idea we were coming, and doesn't give a damn about us." Species extinction is a natural outcome of evolution. Sooner or later our species, like countless others, will become extinct. For the present we appear well positioned for long survival since we lack the two factors that predispose a species for extinction: ecological specialization and a small, localized population. We are ecological generalists, and our huge population is dispersed throughout the planet. Even so, deeply ingrained cultural patterns, supported by powerful interest groups worldwide, jeopardize the survival of civilization and much of the biosphere.

What has happened on Nauru serves as a local example for what is happening all over the earth. A casual observer might say that the Nauruans brought upon themselves the destruction of their island and culture; however, upon closer examination, we see that Nauruans had little power to resist as the world market economy devoured their island. Nauru is an indicator of the long-term results of current trends, and its story is an environmental parable of earth's future.

What will humanity's future be? No one can predict, because biological, physical, and cultural systems are so complex and chaotic. Cultural histories can be informative, however. The story of the Rapa Nui tells us that, even on a small island, negative feedback to a human culture from biodiversity impoverishment can take centuries. Although we cannot determine whether or to what extent the Rapa Nui were aware of the impoverishment, they sealed their fate when they exerted the selection pressures that drove their forests to extinction.

Did the story of the Rapa Nui have to be that way? Could they have made choices that preserved the island's biodiversity and their complex culture? A comparison of the histories of two other Polynesian island cultures, Mangaian and Tikopian, indicates that the Rapa Nui could have made such choices, but the comparison also hints that they took the more likely path.

Mangaia, in the Cook Islands, is a volcanic island of 52 square kilometers, which formed about eighteen million years ago. The central volcanic cone is surrounded by an uplifted reef limestone platform that makes up just over half of the island. This platform, called the Makatea, is about one-third barren rock; the remainder has vegetation and poor soils that present the possibility for marginal agriculture. The Makatea is higher than the inland lowlands and provides catchment basins for streams that drain the volcanic slopes. The island is fringed by a narrow coral reef of low biotic diversity and small biomass; this living matter is exposed at low tide. Although its rocks are now deeply weathered and soil fertility is limited by a lack of elemental phosphorus that oxidizes to form phosphate, at one time the volcanic cone was richly covered by a typical rain forest, in which almost all of the nutrients were in the biomass. The soil was thin, and the biomass was recycled rapidly, and thus, the rain forest preserved biological vitality.

Polynesians arrived about 500 c.e. and brought dogs, pigs, chickens, rats, breadfruit, taro, banana, sweet potato, and coconut, as well as their traditional chief-based society. Slash and burn agriculture and other deforestation over the next 800 years converted the volcanic hillsides into wastelands; erosion of the thin soils from weathered lateritic basalt made forest regeneration impossible. Hunting and habitat destruction led to the extinction of 4 seabird and 13 landbird species. Fruit bats, an important food, were decimated. Marine resources such as mollusks were also overexploited.

Bones deposited from 1000 to 1650 c.e. in the sediments of a rock shelter revealed the number and type of vertebrate species probably eaten during that period. In the oldest zones only fruit bat bones were identified, while in the middle period rat bones dominated, although there were also pig and chicken bones. In the most recent sediment, dating from just before European discovery, rat bones still dominated, while pig bones were absent, chicken bones had decreased dramatically, and a few human bones were present.

The island described by Europeans in the latter part of the eighteenth century was substantially transformed from the one colonized by Polynesians. The upper volcanic slopes of Mangaia, which made up about 24 percent of the island, were degraded fern lands; the lower slopes and valley interiors that constituted about 18 percent of the island were marginally fertile. Most of the soil that had originally been on the volcanic hillsides had eroded into the alluvial basins abutting the Makatea. These basins, which made up only 2 percent of the area, were used by the Mangaians to grow taro in irrigated pond fields, the only productive agriculture on the island.

On Mangaia Europeans did not find a typical Polynesian culture organized around a hereditary chief; rather, the society was ruled by a war chief, the Te Mangaia, who by force had gained control of the irrigated taro-pond fields. Around 1500 C.E., as severely degraded natural ecosystems provided less and less food, the competition for the fertile 2 percent of the island intensified. Rongo, the traditional Polynesian god of agriculture, was culturally transformed into the god of taro and war. The Te Mangaia legitimated his rule by sacrificial offerings of taro roots and human bodies to Rongo. While periodic wars raged over control of the taro-pond fields, most people lived in caves or other defensible refuges. Pushed into the taro fields, the bodies of defeated warriors served as fertilizer. The vanquished were stripped of their taro lands and forced to eke out an existence on the marginal lands of the lower slopes and in the interior valleys. Here was rule by terror; sacrificial victims were stalked by night, and neighboring valleys were continuously raided to secure the resources necessary for sustaining life. Population growth and the consequent biodiversity loss had put the Mangaians in a tight spot.

The history of Tikopia offers a hopeful contrast to Mangaia. Located in the Solomon Islands, it is a tenth the size of Mangaia — its land area is just under 5 square kilometers — and is a much younger volcanic island formed only 80,000 years ago. Unlike Mangaia, its soils are fertile and resilient to weathering. Its surrounding reef is also biologically diverse and well populated. At first the Polynesians who colonized Tikopia about 900 B.C.E. ignored the limits of their island, just as the Mangaians had. They practiced slash and burn agriculture, consumed fruit bats until the bats almost disappeared, caused the extinction of 2 land-bird and 4 sea-bird species and overexploited marine resources to such a degree that mollusk harvests decreased tenfold and fish harvests threefold during the first 800 years of occupation. These losses of protein were replaced by enhanced pig production.

Then, about 100 B.C.E., the pattern of ecosystem destruction and biological impoverishment changed. The intensity of slash and burn agriculture diminished, then stopped. Correlated with the reduction in fire-based agriculture was the appearance of numerous fruit and nut trees that formed an upper canopy and a burgeoning of aroids, yams, and other plants that grow in shade. The Tikopians had replaced their tropical rain forest with a canopied, arbor agriculture that mimicked the ecosystem it replaced; the whole island had become an arbor culture except for a few open places where continuous cultivation of taro and other crops was maintained by intensive mulching. Fish and mollusk resources remained low but stable over a 1,000-year period — 100 B.C.E. to 900 C.E. — and then recovery began. Pigs that had proliferated for almost 2,000 years were eliminated from the island about 1600 C.E., most likely because they were incompatible with multistory arbor culture and because they competed with people for food. The Tikopian population, which had been steadily rising since their arrival, leveled off about 900 C.E. and maintained itself at approximately 1,000 inhabitants.

What happened on Tikopia that gave rise to a society that balanced human needs and population with biological and physical reality yet maintained many attributes of their colonizing culture? Oral tradition says that the Tikopians intentionally and aggressively perpetuated the sustainable society they had created by changing their worldview from one that supported growth and environmental destruction to one that advanced stability. The values of the new worldview were manifested in ritualistic proclamations, believed to be from gods, that advocated the ethics of social harmony, conservation, and, most important, zero population growth. Quarrels between husband and wife were to be settled without violence. Theft, causing a disturbance, and brawling were not acceptable. Conservation of food resources like the coconut or the areca nut was encouraged. The chief's position and his ownership of portions of each orchard were delineated as a means of guaranteeing surplus for the community in times of disaster. Economic forethought necessarily made provisions for culturally required giving, and public welfare was factored into matters of procreation. Tikopians appreciated the necessity of a stable population and did much to maintain it. They understood that intercourse could lead to pregnancy and practiced withdrawal as a means of contraception. Celibacy, abortion, infanticide, suicidal sea voyages by young males, and even expulsion were employed to achieve zero population growth.

It took the Tikopians a long time — more than 1,000 years — to recover some of the richness and resilience in the ecosystems they had impoverished. The choices they made were certainly not easy, and a price was paid. How they came to make these sustaining decisions is forever lost, yet they avoided the fate of other cultures like those found on Rapa Nui and Mangaia.

People live in a finite world. Cultures and economies are now dominant components of earth's biotic enterprise. We have looked at several isolated cultures, especially island cultures, because they allowed us to grasp the real limitations obscured by the larger systems within which we now live. The different histories of these cultures also demonstrate that we can take various paths and that our decisions have profound consequences. As noted by the anthropologist Patrick Kirch: "The human choices and actions that led to particular outcomes and consequences on Easter Island [Rapa Nui], on Mangaia, and on Tikopia — as well as everywhere else on earth — teach us that nothing was inevitable or predetermined. The more modern humanity understands how its predecessors fashioned the earth we have inherited, the better its leaders can be induced to use long-term planning rather than short-term gains as the basis for current action."

Critical decisions with global implications have been made over the past several centuries in Western and world economic culture. The consequences of these choices, now bearing down on us, place us in a position similar to that of the Tikopians 2,000 years ago. We can now observe many of these consequences, among them: multicellular life is experiencing its sixth mass extinction, although the extent is uncertain; about a third of the world's forests have been eliminated, and most of the remaining forests are biologically impoverished regrowth and monoculture tree farms that lack the resilience of primary forests; only a handful of our ocean fisheries are considered healthy; the remaining ones are in decline, in steep decline, or have collapsed; fresh water supplies are inadequate or unsafe for more than half the human population; the current rate of soil erosion exceeds that of soil production (in the United States about 90 percent of the cropland is losing soil above the sustainable rate, and in the last 200 years an estimated 30 percent — 100 million hectares — of farmland has been abandoned because of erosion and salinization or because it has been waterlogged); and in many parts of the world resource scarcity has led to social unrest.

We can see the correlations between the acts that biologically impoverished the Mangaians, the Rapa Nui, and the Nauruans and what is now happening to biodiversity on a planetary scale. Is it possible to alter course? The traditional inhabitants of Nauru, Tikopia, and Ladakh — perhaps because of their small populations and intimate social structures — created local cultures that were economically and environmentally enduring for millennia. By comparison, the world is enormous and culturally complex, and people now act on a global scale. Can we change our globally destructive economic worldview?

World civilization will certainly not go back to living a technologically simple, agrarian life akin to that of traditional Ladakhis, Tikopians, or Nauruans. The myths of our current global economic culture are, in contrast, leading civilization on a path that puts our technologies in the service of a market economy that has scant capacity to preserve biodiversity or ensure human well-being. How shall we decide what to do when we cannot predict the future?

The Tikopians chose more wisely than did the Mangaians or the Rapa Nui. Wisdom dictates we heed the signs and focus all of our efforts on changing to a sustainable pattern of habitation. This enduring habitation will employ many technologies, but for long-term cultural success, these technologies must be wisely chosen to be compatible with preserving biodiversity in the broadest sense. If our current civilization hopes to move along an environmentally sustainable path, it will have to make the market its servant and in the process come full circle to create patterns of living analogous to those of the traditional Tikopians, Ladakhis, and Nauruans, and other societies that, one way or another, learned to live within their biological and physical means.

Chapter Eight

The Chimera of Reality

When we see land as a community to which we belong, we may begin to use it with love and respect. . . .

No important change in ethics was ever accomplished without an internal change in our intellectual emphasis, loyalties, affections, and convictions.

ALDO LEOPOLD, *A Sand County Almanac*

PLEASANT ISLAND is not so pleasant now. The island and its people have been hammered for the past one hundred and fifty years by cultural forces as powerful as the La Niña droughts that profoundly shaped the first pattern of human habitation on Nauru. Guns and alcohol precipitated tremendous social turmoil in its recent history, but the discovery of phosphate in 1900 swept the people of Nauru onto the world stage. Had they forcefully resisted the mining of their homeland at the turn of the century in an effort to preserve the island's natural and cultural heritages, they would have been pushed aside, or simply killed, as were many native peoples in Africa, Australia, the Americas, and islands everywhere. World War I did not greatly affect the Nauruans, but World War II was different. Again they had little say in their destiny, and the outcome was a culture disrupted almost beyond recognition. Finally, with United

156

Nations' support and changing attitudes to colonialism, the Nauruans reclaimed their homeland and the right to make their own choices.

On January 31, 1968, Nauru became an independent nation and the Nauruans had a decision to make. Their negotiators offered their people the attractive opportunity to become truly monetarily wealthy: "In the opinion of the Council [Nauru Local Government Council] the Partner Governments' interests in the phosphate should be confined to these two matters [supply and price], and all other matters affecting the industry should be the exclusive concern of the Nauruan people." And the Australians accepted their loss of a reliable, inexpensive source of phosphate: "The tactics of the Nauruans in recent years is a classic example of what has been described as the 'tyranny of the minority'. But we can hardly begrudge them their victories. We have done very well out of the phosphate and these are the days of reckoning."

Although tremendous momentum disposed them to exploit Topside's phosphate, as the Australians had, the Nauruans had a real opportunity to reclaim their heritage and create an enduring pattern of habitation. About a third of Topside had been mined, which left over two-thirds intact. The island's population was just over 6,000, half of which was Nauruan. In the several years before independence, annual payments to the Nauruans were around $600,000 (Australian) on phosphate revenues from export of 1,500,000 tons of phosphate ore. The world market value per ton was about $12 (Australian) with a per ton cost of production of just under $6 (Australian). At this rate of extraction the remaining phosphate, an estimated 60 million tons, would last about forty years and give them an annual profit of at least $9,000,000 (Australian).

The Nauruans faced a difficult choice. No one who understands the history of Nauru under colonial rule and then trusteeship could fault them for electing to reap the financial rewards of mining the island's remaining phosphate. In addition, it was not clear to them, or perhaps to any of their advisors, that their growing participation in world markets would lead them to adopt an immensely destructive pattern of habitation. One can argue that their decision to continue mining phosphate was the best possible, because they would avoid the fate of their financially impoverished island neighbors and because they would have the wealth to participate wholeheartedly in the world economy. Even so, mining had already irrevocably degraded over a third of their island, and mining the remaining phosphate would utterly destroy Topside — 80 percent of Nauru. Was trading the biological and physical bases of a lifestyle in order to gain a few more dollars befitting their hard-won independence?

Let us consider, however, the outcome if, after much agonizing, the Nauruan people had decided to save as much of Topside as possible. Using only a part of the tremendous phosphate wealth still buried under Topside, they would have had the financial security to establish new economic and political relations with the rest of the world as an independent, self-sufficient people. They would have had to mine enough phosphate to settle obligations agreed to in the transfer of the phosphate industry, but that would have taken only a few years, after which time they could have reduced mining operations. In the early 1960s they lived quite well on their salaries and on the $600,000 (Australian) the British Phosphate Commissioners provided. If the Nauruans had reduced mining 90 percent, they would have been able to maintain their standard of living with an annual profit in excess of $900,000 (Australian).

By scaling back the annual rate of phosphate extraction to 150,000 tons, they would have gained flexibility and time to address the formidable challenge of re-creating durable lifestyles. Their goal could have been for Nauru to provide as many of the basic necessities of life as possible. With reduced phosphate output, many of the 3,000 foreigners could have left Nauru, which would have reduced the excessively large population. Within perhaps ten years the Nauruans could have learned all aspects of phosphate mining, and the remaining foreigners associated with mining could have left. At the same time the Nauruans could have made a long-term plan, perhaps a one hundred-year plan, to return to a population size compatible with the island's resources, a number close to the pre-European 1,000 to 1,500 people.

Analyses of species numbers on other islands, a field of study called

"island biogeography," indicate that with about two-thirds of Topside still in its pre-mining condition, 90 percent of the native species of animals, microbes, and plants were still present in 1968. These biological reserves would have been sufficient to repopulate mined-out areas as they were restored. Perhaps the ships returning to Nauru for more phosphate could have brought fill and topsoil. In any event, they could have planned to restore land faster than it would be mined until, after fifty years, mining could cease because all of Topside would be either filled and being restored, or intact. This fifty-year scenario of annually mining 150,000 tons means that about half of Topside could have remained unmined forever. It is unclear how the restoration efforts would have fared, but even if recovery would take hundreds to thousands of years, restoration would have been under way, while the intact areas would have been available for other uses. Although additional mining would always be possible, it would be contingent on long-term preservation of sustainable habitation.

The Nauruans could have restored the coral reef, coconut and pandanus trees, as well as other biological resources, and gradually begun to use them as in the past. Over time they would have decided which technologies are appropriate for the pattern of enduring habitation they would create. In a few decades a larger and larger fraction of the population would be fed, housed, and clothed, using the resources of the local ecosystems until the island could once again support its population. During this period the profits from mining spent on importing food and materials would decrease. Nauruans could have added this savings to the trust funds as an income source — a financial cushion for their interactions with the rest of the world when mining would cease.

Had the Nauruan leaders and people chosen a path in 1968 similar to the one just outlined — a most difficult and unlikely choice — they would now be thirty years into re-creating a durable pattern of habitation. Instead, they followed an economic path that inadvertently led to the abandonment of a local culture for a homogenous market economy. Today, Nauruan choices are more limited and their future far less certain than it was thirty years ago: the phosphate is gone; Topside is totally devastated; and the Nauruan population has doubled. As the Reverend

James Aingimea, the eighty-four-year-old minister of the Nauru Congregational Church said in 1995, "I wish we'd never discovered that phosphate. I wish Nauru could be like it was before. When I was a boy, it was so beautiful. There were trees. It was green everywhere, and we could eat the fresh coconuts and breadfruit. Now I see what has happened here, and I want to cry."

In North American publications some westerners express moral indignation at the Nauruans' plight: "Here was Nauru with a history of such affluence. But having dug out all their island for the phosphate so stupidly, they stupidly spent their money as well. They need to take the blame themselves. They are in a lot of trouble because they have not saved for a rainy day," and "Nauru's decline has to do with human nature. It's what happens when incentives are taken away and people don't have to work." But what is the reality of the Nauruans' situation? They did not bring Europeans to their island, nor did they create the market economy that physically destroyed the island and destabilized their civilization. These things happened as a result of two influential beliefs in Western culture: that native cultures are expendable for progress and that natural environments exist for the purposes of making money and supporting progress by feeding the growing market economy. The Nauruans had an enduring pattern of habitation prior to 1800; therefore, these failures should not be ascribed to them but to the market economy.

Nauru has served as a crystal ball in which to view the consequences of beliefs and actions prevalent in our market-based world. We can appreciate how difficult, if not impossible, it would be for the current population of Nauruans to live at this time on their island's impoverished biological and physical resources. It is certainly not prudent to denude the entire earth the way Nauru, Banaba, Beijing, London, Mangaia, Manhattan Island, Mexico City, Moscow, Rapa Nui, and so many other places have been denuded.

Humans lived as integrated components of local ecosystems for several million years. With the advent of agriculture we gained the capacity to acquire more resources from local ecosystems for our use. Over the past

10,000 years, as agriculture came to predominate throughout the world, people, by way of trade and ever more sophisticated technologies, moved beyond the limitations of local ecosystems. Within the past century, though, the situation has changed again. Our presence — our numbers and the consequences of our technologies, including agriculture — is so pervasive that we are pressing hard on the limits of the global ecosystem.

While many technologies have assaulted biodiversity on a grand scale, it is certain that people will not easily relinquish those things considered essential to the good life. Since technology has facilitated the present round of global destruction, we have little hope that technology alone will permit biodiversity to flourish — with the market as our master, technology is the handmaiden of this destruction. The challenge is to adopt technologies compatible with enduring habitation, although identifying such technologies takes a long time. We tend to concentrate on positive attributes in order to bring a new technology into use as quickly as possible — only to discover the negative, unintended consequences after the technology has been widely adopted. The chemical revolution is replete with examples — DDT, CFCs, and the myriad chemicals that mimic hormones. The gasoline-powered car has been fantastically seductive because of the personal independence and convenience it provides, yet the environmental devastation is visible from space — cities of roads, parking lots, shopping malls, junkyards — and the resulting destruction of neighborhood businesses and community is lamentable. Unintended consequences are inevitable, but the wisdom of allowing the marketplace to make decisions about what is compatible with sustainable habitation is questionable. Although our record for adopting viable technologies — those that function within the context of preserving natural resources — is poor, it is theoretically possible that specific technologies and enduring habitation could be compatible.

In societies such as the Rapa Nui and the Mangaians, their cultural myths found expression in behavior that was incompatible with long-term stability. In these societies the environmental changes caused by deforestation and erosion were gradual and probably imperceptible to the inhabitants. When problems finally became apparent, reassuring, deeply ingrained myths most likely convinced people that a change in behavior was unnecessary. In 1200 C.E. a person on Rapa Nui who noted the loss of forest and birds and recommended limited cutting and replanting would have been marginalized as a heretic — bigger statues were on the way and surely the gods would continue to provide. But Rapa Nui technology did not resolve the problems resulting from the impoverished biological and physical conditions on the island, but rather exacerbated those conditions, as well as the gradual social disintegration.

Over millennia peoples in the Western sphere have relied on their cultural myths to enable them to adapt to environmental and historical vicissitudes, and now many in this sphere who participate in world economic culture are challenged by the knowledge that these myths are no longer adaptive. All peoples and cultures have deeply held beliefs, which are exceedingly refractory to change despite overwhelming empirical evidence contradicting them. This may sound like a harsh judgment, yet history is replete with stories of our propensity to endorse improbable beliefs and to act on them. Even people of the greatest insight, sagacity, and common sense harbor the beliefs of their culture. Like the Rapa Nui, who created bigger and bigger statues to appease the gods, today's world political leaders clamor for more economic growth as a means of maintaining civilization and guaranteeing human well-being. Our present reality is truly chimeric: over several millennia we have come to tightly embrace a worldview upon which we still base our actions and behavior, yet within the last several hundred years, all of the major components of this worldview have been demonstrated untenable or false.

How Shall We Proceed?

Where is the blueprint for a pattern of habitation that will make humans happy and support our species' existence in perpetuity? In all honesty, it does not exist — we have to create it. In this process of creation, ancient and modern cultures may reveal general directions toward which we can reorient our economic worldview to promote a sustainable and thus enduring human future.

The histories of failed and of successful cultures provide scenarios for destroying or preserving local ecosystems. Scaling up patterns of durable habitation from small, isolated cultures to a world culture is not easy, nor is scaling down the expanding global economy to a pattern of small, enduring units. Our difficulty is developing techniques and procedures, using long-lived sustainable cultures as models, to change existing cultures so that they will retain or acquire the qualities underlying the endurance of these models as the global aggregate of cultures is created and perpetuated.

Science's story compels us to act differently than we have in recent times: to establish incentives in order to direct human behavior so that it is consistent with preserving physical and biological resources. People in some traditional cultures act in this way, supported by myths, honed by trial and error over millennia, that encourage environmentally rational behavior and that acknowledge spiritual affinity with the rest of creation. Today, most of us in the West have lost even the vestiges of such traditions that respect and revere nature, but if we can recapture these attitudes, our actions and policies will surely change. These qualities for the Australian aborigines were in "the Dreaming — that timeless epoch of creativity that gave form to the diversity of life, set in motion nature's cycles, and left its enduring imprint upon the earth's crust — all species, including kindred humans, were subtly entwined within a transcendent web of meaning that renders eternally sacred the processes, places, and personages of the natural world." Science has reaffirmed this wisdom of the ancients: enduring habitation will come to a world whose inhabitants live in a way that befits the finite and fragile earth.

The quality and quantity of information gained over the past few centuries is phenomenal. We can now describe many of our environmental problems in exceptional detail, but information alone is insufficient to guide civilization through the current biodiversity bottleneck. We need wisdom in the form of new ethics, values, and behaviors for our technological society. And the ethics we need will have to conform to the biological and physical realities elucidated by the natural and social sciences, yet these disciplines can present inappropriate choices by being surrogates for a wiser ethical system. This is dangerously true for economics, where choices are now based on monetary values almost exclusively within the confines of a econocentric worldview.

Our economic system has delivered a phenomenal level of material wealth and a dazzling array of creature comforts to a sizable minority of the world's population. Yet the market system is not based on values that respect life in general and human life in particular. The price-based market system is like the medieval Jewish Golem, a magical, robotlike creature made from clay and given life—a useful creation if carefully instructed, watched, and controlled but clumsy and apt to chop off your head or crush you if you are not mindful. The Golem was intended to be a servant, just as the market should be our servant. We, however, have allowed market-based values to dominate civilization and to threaten dire consequences. Our world civilization and its global economy are based on beliefs incompatible with enduring habitation of the earth: that everything has been put on earth for our use, that resources not used to meet our needs are wasted and resources are unlimited, that rewards must be related to economic production, that people are exclusively selfish and acquisitive, that scarcity and inequality are natural conditions, and that the biosphere is a subset of the economy.

Weak or strong, sustainable development as a purely economic concept falls short of policies that lead to durable habitation, because people do not have the opportunity to create choices compatible with environmental preservation. Sustainable habitation consists of more than fostering market activity, which does not concern itself with maintaining local, much less global, biological, or social integrity.

Markets and Energy

In many critical situations, people are not given appropriate choices; the wrong question hardly ever elicits a pertinent response. Among a host of interconnected elements—technology, population, lifestyle, habitat destruction, development, consumption, climate change — each of which needs to be addressed, energy illustrates this conundrum of the wrong question. The market economics of energy is driven by the relative prices of energy sources, not by principles of sustainability. These prices do not indicate which source will promote persistent biological integrity and long-term human well-being. And so the price-based market cannot be relied upon to ask the question whose response addresses sustainability.

According to the World Energy Council the world economy used the equivalent of 27 billion barrels of oil in 1960, 65 billion barrels in 1990, and will use up to 126 billion barrels in 2020. Fossil fuels accounted for over 82 percent of total energy used in 1960 and 77 percent in 1990, and they are projected to account for 77 percent in 2020. Exclusive of hydrological power, which is not necessarily renewable because of silting, all renewable sources of energy accounted for 15 percent in 1960 and 13 percent in 1990 and are projected to account for 12 percent in 2020. These energy sources have been allocated by markets primarily as a function of price, which reflects substantial subsidies, hidden and otherwise. The numbers indicate that the current market system has opted, and will continue to opt, to run the economy with fossil fuels.

Ecosystems and individual species run on energy flows, and economic systems are no different. The phenomenal economic growth of the twentieth century has been driven by harnessing fossil fuels. For most of the century a one-to-one relation existed between the economy's growth and the growth rate of fossil fuel use. The undeniable contribution of fossil fuels to our present well-being and their adverse environmental effects illustrate the conflict between short-term individual self-interest and long-term social interests. Fossil fuels are currently an economically inexpensive source of energy. For most of the twentieth century, except for the 1970s and early 1980s, fossil fuel prices adjusted for inflation have declined, and real gasoline prices have never been lower. Despite mounting evidence of the adverse environmental impacts of fossil-fuel extraction, transport, and use, not only has consumption grown tremendously but it has also replaced benign sources of energy — solar energy and a host of conservation technologies.

Fossil fuels are stocks of reduced carbon representing millions of years of photosynthetically acquired solar energy that has been removed from the biosphere for hundreds of millions of years. Human activities are now releasing this store of carbon at rates many times greater than current assimilation rates. As a consequence, natural processes are not removing this additional input, and carbon dioxide is rapidly accumulating in the atmosphere. This higher carbon dioxide concentration influences essentially every ecosystem in unknown and unpredictable ways because of its influence on plant growth. In addition, climatologists' claims that greenhouse gas production is forcing climate change are not new: the Swedish chemist Svante Arrhenius predicted it in 1896.

Although the market cannot factor in all of the economic or environmental aftereffects of employing a certain energy source — comprehensive short-term feedback is lacking and some consequences are unknowable — it can help to allocate energy sources. Decisions on which energy sources to develop or use should be based on physical — atmospheric, oceanographic, geologic — and biological data, and markets should allocate energy within the constraints defined by these data. Unfortunately, the world's big energy-using countries have developed a subsidized market to use fossil-fuel energy and, to a lesser degree, nuclear power, but they have not seriously addressed the repercussions of using these sources.

Many analyses conclude that it is possible to power the world's economies without using fossil fuel or nuclear energy. Two simplified examples illustrate the possibilities, but they should not be taken as a panacea for our energy problems. In California and other sunny parts of the world, solar energy reaching the ground is over 20 million kilowatt hours per hectare per year. A trough system in California concentrates sunlight on oil, and the heated oil is used to make electricity by means of steam turbine–driven generators; this arrangement can collect 3 million kilowatt hours per hectare per year. During its projected 25-year life, one collector provides 50 times the amount of energy it takes to make the collector. This primitive solar technology could produce all the energy now used in the world if concentrators were placed in 100 million hectares of desert — less than 10 percent of the earth's desert area. Another calculation indicates that all energy consumed in the Midwest of the United States could be produced from local windmills. Although the infrastructure for a solar world is not yet in place, it could be created in a decade or so. Remember, the infrastructure for today's oil-based world did not exist less than a century ago.

People would be prudent to choose solar energy over fossil-fuel energy, but markets cannot make this choice. If we choose to substitute solar energy for fossil-fuel energy, we will no longer add fossil fuel– derived carbon dioxide to the atmosphere. We could also choose to reduce energy consumption to curtail its negative effects on biodiversity. An aggressive ten- or twenty-year plan would allow us to run the human world not only on solar energy but also on much less total energy. We could simply decide to do so and then create incentives, market or otherwise, to make it happen.

More Is Less

The cherished beliefs that more people and more consumption are desirable are now untenable. Global civilizations will thrive over the long haul only when we citizens of the world come to terms with the myriad population problems that face us. The population issue is technically and ethically complicated because the number of people that can live sustainably in an area is tightly correlated with lifestyle and the economic system that supports it. The global economy as constructed requires continual growth for optimal functioning, and this generates a substantial subculture that encourages, even dictates, an extravagant lifestyle that per capita uses an inordinate amount of resources. In the long run, a lavish existence — whose attributes include big cars and vans for transportation;

goods originating thousands of miles away; large homes, second homes, yachts, and recreational vehicles; and resort-style vacations in faraway places — has huge environmental effects that result in a much smaller carrying capacity for an area than a lifestyle with a quite different consumption pattern that includes travel by bicycle and mass transit; a diet of locally grown grains, fruits, vegetables, and other foods; simple but adequate homes; and local vacations. In short, the area of ecologically productive land required to support a person living extravagantly on the global bounty is much larger than the area needed for a more modest lifestyle supported primarily by local resources. Thus, the population issue is not merely a numbers question because it embodies the environmental consequences of lifestyle, as well as other issues such as equity, that we have not considered.

Historical analyses of preindustrial human habitation indicate that functional boundaries are often associated with a biological or geological feature like a watershed. These natural boundaries divide the landscape into units that have significance for its inhabitants. Each region has a carrying capacity connected to its resources and how they are employed. Trade and then industrialization have obscured boundaries and enlarged the apparent carrying capacity of most regions. Consequently, the entire planet's ecological and material wealth is capable in the present of supporting 6 billion people; over the long haul, though, it may be foolish for a region to depend heavily on outside resources.

An example from the Pacific islands warns us about the relation between trade and regional stability. In the remote southeastern region of Polynesia three islands — Henderson, Mangareva, and Pitcairn — initiated a trading network about 1,000 C.E. that lasted about 450 years. Each island lacked items present on other islands. Mangareva was well endowed biologically but had no source of high-quality stone needed for adzes and other tools. Pitcairn had two quarries, one that yielded volcanic glass for sharp tools and another brimming with fine-grained basalt that made excellent adzes. Pitcairn, in comparison, had poor soils and a reefless coastline that limited marine resources. While Mangareva and

Pitcairn were volcanic islands, Henderson was a coral island with no sources of stone tools, no reliable freshwater supply, and trees too small to fashion into oceangoing canoes. It did have spectacular beaches for vacationing, birds with beautiful red feathers that were a luxury item, and an annual appearance of egg-laying green turtles that provided a consistent source of turtle meat, a prized delicacy. Trade among the islands became brisk.

This arrangement worked well for several hundred years and permitted the populations to grow to well over 1,000 on Mangareva, about 100 on Pitcairn, and perhaps two dozen on Henderson. By 1500 trade had ceased, and in 1606, when Henderson was found by Europeans, it was uninhabited, as was Pitcairn in 1790. In 1797 Europeans arrived at Mangareva and found a situation similar to Rapa Nui and Mangaia. The people of Mangareva had destroyed the biodiversity base that supported them and their trading partners; and all three island civilizations went down together. This is a cautionary tale for the current global economy, which is accelerating interdependencies among its members and destroying local biodiversity to support large populations everywhere and high-consumption lifestyles in industrialized countries.

The Tikopians had stabilized their population and maintained enough biodiversity to provide for their needs, but their backs were against the wall. They had converted their entire island into a garden. Celibacy, contraception, abortion, infanticide, and the occasional putting to sea of members of the society indicate that the Tikopians had little margin for error in their system. This was the price they had to pay for stability and for waiting so long to implement zero population growth. At the same time, the wisdom of ancient decisions can be seen in Tikopia's twentieth-century history. When a Christian mission came in the 1920s, many population control measures were abandoned, and the population grew from 1,200 in 1929 to 2,000 in 1952. Cyclones in 1952 and 1953 ravaged half of the island's crops, and famine ensued. Only relief supplies prevented a worse disaster. The council of chiefs now allows just 1,100 people to live on Tikopia, and overflow moves to neighboring islands in the Solomons.

We may continue along our path of converting all arable areas into cities, suburbs, and industrial farms. Our current worldview supports the viability of these actions, yet these conversions will lead to the simplification and therefore the impoverishment of the remaining mature ecosystems on arable land, thereby accelerating the ongoing mass extinction. Such a choice is inconsistent with prudent thinking on a global scale and would result in an enormous reduction in much of the earth's remaining biodiversity. Of equal importance, industrial agriculture is just not sustainable in the long run. Wisdom dictates we do as the Tikopians did: develop an ecosystem-based agriculture and achieve zero and then negative population growth as soon as possible.

If it is ill-advised to convert the whole planet into an industrial farm, how much of the earth need we preserve? The 3 percent of the earth's land area set aside in national parks is insufficient for preserving biodiversity. While working to respect the requirements of local communities, Costa Rica has allocated about a quarter of its land as wildlife preserves, and it hopes to do more. If we were to mimic on a global scale what Costa Rica has done, we would be moving toward maintaining biodiversity. In the long run a goal of setting aside a third to a half of the landmass, free of economic exploitation, would be consistent with the proportion many ecologists consider necessary to curb biodiversity loss. In addition, because numerous aquatic habitats — estuaries, intertidal areas, coastal waters, coral reefs — have been severely disrupted and impoverished by people, it would be wise to preserve and restore expanses of the aquatic environment so they perform the functions necessary to sustain our activities.

Can We Change?

We have attempted to identify the core of our global environmental conundrum as well as to suggest appropriate directions that might be taken to avoid the collapse of our global civilization. We should not forget, however, the many hopeful signs observed everywhere; in addition, innumerable people who understand that our myths no longer square with the natural sciences are addressing the reality we face. Over twenty years ago the Land Institute in Salina, Kansas, began to develop a sustainable agriculture (Natural Systems Agriculture), based upon prairie ecology, for the prairies of the United States. The Natural Step Program, started in Sweden about six years ago and now spread to the entire world, has the goal of helping companies to function like ecosystems by recycling everything and flowing energy efficiently. The Malpai Borderlands Project in New Mexico and Arizona, where local ranchers came together several years ago to work with all parties to preserve their way of life and the land, while still making a living from ranching, shows that local communities can cooperate and that they are key to bioregional stability. In the Nature Conservancy's Last Great Places project, people work to combine human habitation and ecosystem preservation. New York State's Adirondack Park has had over a hundred years' experience in making wilderness preservation inclusive of human presence. The bioregional movement provides clear evidence that people are trying to figure out how humans can live well with the resources of their region. For over twenty-five years the Population Institute's programs have positively illustrated that human population growth can be reversed with dignity and respect by emphasizing education and political involvement and, most important, by addressing each situation individually. And numerous religious communities of every faith have initiated programs that emphasize the value and sacredness of all of God's creation.

These few examples come from an enormous and ever growing list of people, organizations, and actions, yet the overwhelming inertia of our econocentric worldview is daunting. We will have to use all our present and future knowledge — anthropological, chemical, ecological, economic, geological, historical, political, philosophical, psychological, sociological, theological — to learn to inhabit the planet in a sustainable and civilized manner. At the same time, we appreciate the difficulty in effecting the prodigious changes required of our econocentric culture, because its core myths are based upon stories once held as truths and because of the inherent obstacles to a culture's changing its core myths and the beliefs and actions evoked by them. In ancient Greece the Ladder of Nature organized the world in a rational way, just as in the medieval West the placement of angels, the heavens, and God above the Ladder with the earth as the center of the universe constituted a coherent worldview. The linear concept of progress and the notion that the wild world needs to be tamed and improved coincided with contemporary understandings in the centuries following the Middle Ages.

In the last several centuries the natural sciences and other branches of human knowledge — among them, history, anthropology, and archaeology — have generated the most universally consistent explanations for how the world works. These explanations, often supported by ancient wisdom not well represented in the current econocentric worldview, have established that our trajectory is economically and environmentally unsustainable. Thus, the world's cultures are in a tumultuous period because the old myths of economic growth and never-ending material progress are no longer believable, but the new stories have not yet been culturally enshrined. It is unclear how or when this momentous shift from an *econo*centric to an *eco*centric worldview will be accomplished. One thing is certain, though: as on Rapa Nui or Mangaia, natural laws, especially those of biology, will take a toll on current cultures as they have on past cultures whose impoverished ecosystems could no longer provide the materials and functions necessary to maintain them. The Tikopians saw the writing on the wall, and by exercising restraint, they transformed their unsustainable culture into an enduring one. This is the challenge we face, and thousands of activities now under way indicate that people are attempting to effect the transition.

We have told many stories to stimulate thought about who we are and how we have inhabited the earth. Like biodiversity, human diversity is phenomenally rich, varied, and in a word, extraordinary. Although we are all constrained by the tiny fraction of the gene pool given by our parents, the aggregate potential of the genes expressed in groups of people is immense. In principle we can develop virtually any imaginable culture that accounts for our genetic inheritance. The challenge is to create cultures that respect the whole creation, that bring out the best human qualities, and that are compatible with equitable and enduring habitation.

The Nauruans missed an opportunity in 1968 to begin to re-create an enduring culture while they had the biological and economic wealth to do so. We now have a chance to recognize and act on the knowledge that we are subject to biological laws and that we have already exceeded the limits of sustainable resource exploitation and abuse. The story of how the world came to be the way it is calls for a reoriented worldview directed toward enduring habitation. To choose and then walk the path to an enduring civilization will not be easy — and perhaps we need some catastrophe to set us firmly on that path. We are humbled, even daunted, when we understand that humans are merely one small part of the giant biotic adventure occurring on Earth. As others have noted, one planet, one experiment. The path will be traveled but once.

Coda

————

AS I SCRAMBLED to finish preparations for my talk at Grinnell College's spring symposium titled "What Is the Earth Worth?" a conversation with Jeff Gersh, an environmental video producer, thrust the subconscious nag center stage. He had read the latest draft of this book and bluntly said, "The story of Nauru has yet to be written. Go there for a year and connect with the people. Understand what is going on by being there." Jeff was right. The book had been written and only fine-tuning remained, but although my coauthor, John Gowdy, had visited Nauru once, we knew little firsthand about the Nauruans, who were about to enter a future without phosphate. In a matter of a week my travel agent was figuring out how to get me and my wife, Mary, there.

Our agent, Elana, easily found Air Nauru and made reservations for us, but when their listing disappeared from the electronic ticketing network, she got very nervous. A few phone calls and several faxes later, she was still nervous but believed that she had reservations for us on the weekly flight from Fiji to Nauru. Although she was unable to finalize our reservations at the Menen Hotel, she gave me a fax indicating that they were expecting us for the month of July. Then, just days before our departure, I received a fax from the Nauruan secretary of external affairs, Angie Itsimaera, telling us to delay our travel until we had government permission to visit as an author and potential video maker. We exchanged faxes with the secretary right up to the day of departure without resolution, which further added to our anxiety. Since our air tickets were refundable only with a substantial penalty, we decided to go to Nauru anyway.

This flight was an airline adventure. Our two-hour connection time in Los Angeles became twenty minutes. Thanks to a thoughtful airline ticketing agent in Chicago, we were put in first class, so we could exit immediately on arrival, and we ran the distance from domestic to international terminals in just under nine minutes. At the QANTAS desk we were told the flight was closed, but our exasperation, and perspiration, motivated a check and another run, this time with the QANTAS agent to the about-to-be-closed gate. But our luggage did not fare so well — it arrived on Fiji three days later, on the day before our departure for Nauru. Was all of this prelude for what was to come?

From the airplane window Nauru looked pretty green and, well, like a pleasant island. At immigration and customs the woman official asked us, "Transit?"

"No, we've come for a four-week visit."

"On Nauru! Government papers? Authorization?"

I wanted to say I had written to the president — I had — and he was anticipating our visit — he wasn't — but I suspected the humor might be lost. "We have communicated with the government and have hotel reservations." I silently blessed Elana as I handed the woman the fax from the Menen Hotel. She took the fax and our passports to confer with superiors. She returned. "Okay, but we need the fax for our records."

As we walked into the humid, tropical sunshine in search of transport, I hoped the hotel had our reservation, but we were on Nauru so it didn't really matter.

The next morning as we walked toward the commercial center, a Nauruan in his mid sixties stopped his car and leaned out of the window.

"New on the island ... want a lift?" We accepted and hopped in the backseat. He introduced himself as Alfred Dick.

John and his wife, Linda, told us that during their visit they had found no fresh fruits or vegetables and no orange juice for breakfast. When Mary spied the large bag of huge oranges on the front seat, she immediately exclaimed, "Beautiful oranges! Where did you get them?"

Without hesitation, Alfred grabbed two oranges, offering them to her. "Have some."

And this happened again and again throughout our visit: meals, produce, favors, and even invitations to family affairs like weddings and first-birthday parties. We quickly learned what I had read was true — Nauruans are generous and personal requests are granted.

Within our first hours on Nauru, Alfred Dick had given us a profound lesson: We are all humans with physical characteristics that make each of us unique, but behind the physical is the cultural. Just as we are defined as a species by human nature with its deep evolutionary roots that have been influenced by gene-culture interplay, we are individually defined in a most profound way by the culture through which we initially come to interpret the world in which we live. I am a North American of European descent — I cannot see the world as a Nauruan. This situation is exacerbated by the fact that I do not speak Nauruan. Although every Nauruan we met spoke English, it is a second language. Personal discourse among Nauruans is in Nauruan — it is the language that shapes their understanding of the world and connects them socially. As a consequence, much of Nauruan culture was hidden from me and most of the other foreigners on Nauru. It is thus with great reservation that I attempt to convey to you my observations of Nauru and the Nauruan people. I have tried my best, but I will be off the mark in some places and just plain wrong in others.

My concern is heightened by the fact that the modern North American cultural perspective makes quick work of the Nauruan situation — propagated in articles in the popular press like *Reader's Digest* and syndicated columns that measure Nauruans against Western norms. These analyses conclude with dispatch that Nauruans by omission or commission, only have themselves to blame for the crisis on their island and certainly deserve whatever catastrophes are visited upon them. In my view these assessments of Nauruans are wrong. I believe these analyses are off the mark, not because they misidentify the proximal causes — inappropriate investments, insufficient savings, minimal incentive to work, failure to create an economy capable of supporting their comprehensive welfare state — but because they fail to consider ultimate causes: Nauruan cultural history, the character of equatorial Pacific island habitation, and the fundamental incompatibility between Nauruan perspectives as an island culture and the global market economy.

I felt it was important to walk on Nauru so as to be physically connected to the land and its life — to sense everything slowly — to hear the wind, to touch the leaves, to feel the sunshine, heat, and humidity. I wanted to grasp in some small way what Nauru was like before westernization, as well as to experience the island as it is now. And I wished to experience this place as a Nauruan might, to hear the pounding surf twenty-four hours a day and to be exposed to tropical temperatures that average 28°C every month of the year.

Nauru is a small island — we leisurely walked around it one morning in four hours — and most of the activity is situated on the several-hundred-meter-wide coastal strip. As in my hometown of Troy, New York, few people on Nauru walk any distance, so Mary and I stood out not only because we looked different, but also because we walked everywhere. Numerous times people stopped to offer rides. Some would pass us as we walked, turn their cars around, and come back to offer a lift.

Nauru has two hotels: the Od-N-Aiwo (privately owned and located on the western side of the island in the commercial area) and the Menen Hotel (government owned and located on the eastern side of the island in a residential area just south of Anibare Bay). When Alfred Dick picked us up, we were headed for the Od-N-Aiwo. John and Linda had recommended it as the place to stay because of its central location, but we couldn't make contact from Troy. The Od-N-Aiwo had neat, clean rooms that were less expensive than those at the Menen. We decided, however, money and convenience were less important than ambiance and people. The guests at the Menen — foreigners who provided a wide range of expertise to Nauru (financial managers, lawyers, scientists), foreign teachers hired by the Education Department, Air Nauru's pilots and flight engineers, and businesspeople — could give us insights into the Nauruan situation we would be hard pressed to gain on our own in a brief four-week visit.

It was afternoon on our first full day by the time we had exchanged our U.S. dollars for Australian dollars (the currency used on Nauru), looked around, eaten a snack, and headed for the interior. We had been walking for about an hour and a half on a hot, dusty road that curved through ninety years of mined-out wasteland toward the center of the island when a pickup truck stopped, and Halsey leaned out the window offering a ride. Named after Admiral Bull Halsey of World War II fame, Halsey Capelle was acting production superintendent for Nauru Phosphate Corporation (NPC). He was about my height — 5' 8" — but with the stockier Nauruan build. Prior to his current position he had worked on ships as an engineer and had been all over the world including the United States. His three children were in school on Fiji while he and his wife lived on Nauru.

We rode with him to the loading area in the center of the island, where he parked his pickup in the shade of a tree out of the mid-afternoon sun. Like Alfred Dick, he spoke excellent English and he seemed pleased to talk with us. We stood in the shade overlooking the loading area while Halsey explained the operation. A conveyor belt moved recently mined phosphate ore up a tower to a man who removed coral rock that was intermingled with the phosphate. The ore went through pulverizing rollers and then onto another belt that eventually dumped it into a gondola car for transport to the phosphate facility near the Od-N-Aiwo. I asked permission to take pictures — he had no objections.

He then drove us to the major area of active mining. In the early days

Chinese and other foreign laborers had dug the ore with hand tools from between the pinnacles and carried their filled baskets through previously dug coral canyons to conveyor belts. Now, mechanical grapples scooped out the phosphate to be hauled by trucks to the loading area. The scene looked just like the picture on the dust jacket of Christopher Weeramantry's book *Nauru: Environmental Damage under International Trusteeship*. Starkly beautiful but ominous, the naked landscape of whitish tan pinnacles lay silent against the drone of the grapple and the barely perceptible sound of distant surf. We stood silently and just watched.

As we drove back Halsey asked if we wanted a view of everything. On the south side of the loading area we drove up a 20-meter high hill covered with scrub vegetation and a few small trees. From "the-top-of-the-world" we could see the entire island and ocean on all sides. This vantage point was created by the pileup of the thin layer of topsoil that had been scraped from Topside to expose the phosphate ore. We chatted about our families, the origins of our names (my middle name is Nimitz — my mother was related to Fleet Admiral Chester Nimitz), and just how difficult it is to keep the decrepit mining machinery operational. I asked him about restored areas and restoration projects — he said he knew of none.

The active and recently mined sites were moonscapes like areas we had seen at Death Valley in California and in the Badlands of South Dakota — no soil, no life, just granular debris, rocks, and coral pinnacles that were virtually impossible to traverse. From the top of the world the devastation radiated in all directions. But it was muted by the green of regrowth and the oxidized gray of the exposed coral pinnacles that stood like thousands of stoic sentries witnessing some sacred rite. I could almost hear the surf against the blue sky, but the wind's constant sound blended with the clanging of machinery and conveyor belts to focus my mind on the ritual of disassembling the land — the island and its once durable aggregate of life. Indeed, the top of Nauru had been sent to Australia, New Zealand, and beyond to make deserts bloom, while the intricate web of the island's life had been reduced to the few hardy survivors that could thrive in the rubble of human occupation.

We thanked Halsey as he dropped us at a store, Elizabeth's Garden, one of the few places that had any books. There I purchased two books about Nauru that I had not already read. It was about four-thirty, and we were hot and thirsty. Our water bottles were not empty, but Mary wanted juice and I thought ice cream would hit the spot. We finished our snacks as we passed the Aiwo Primary School at the west end of the airport runway.

In the morning we had gone along the north side of the runway, so we decided to walk the south side by the parliament and government offices. The modern, attractive, and well-kept government complex contrasted with the Yaren Primary School just to the east that must have lost its sparkle decades ago. A bit further we came to a picnic area with a spectacular view of the reef and the ocean beyond. No one was there, nor did it look inviting — broken glass littered the ground and some of the tables needed fixing. As we neared the end of the runway, a car stopped and Bruce Graham, a New Zealander who had seen us on yesterday's flight from Fiji, offered a ride. Bruce, a chemist running his own environmental consulting firm located in New Zealand, was working on a contract involving a number of islands and their toxic wastes. He introduced his government host and driver, Pene Agadia, a Nauruan environmental officer in the Ministry of Island Development and Industry. We chatted about our reasons for being here as we drove to the Menen and departed with arrangements to have dinner with Bruce.

On the equator sunrises and sunsets are at the same time, twelve hours apart — 7 A.M. and 7 P.M. for Nauru — so the sun was setting when we walked onto the patio for the buffet dinner. A day in the open had whetted our appetites for the feast of fresh greens, marinated raw fish, pasta salad, grilled fish, chicken, and beef, with Jell-O and flan for desert. The patio was just meters from the tidal pools of the reef. The breeze was pleasantly warm as we watched the rising moon and listened to the continuous rolling of the waves at the reef's edge.

At dinner we were joined by Glen Jamieson, a retired Australian engineer who was volunteering through the Nauruan government to help the Menen Hotel with their technical problems. Glen had spent most of his life in the Pacific islands and was halfway through his five-month assignment at the Menen. Glen told of the problems he was addressing — the sewage treatment system that was dumping raw sewage into the ocean, air-conditioning units that had stopped working, the broken swimming pool–chlorinating system, and the half-dozen or so sea-transport containers filled with as yet unsorted miscellany from the now gutted Nauruan-owned hotel in Melbourne. Unlike some of the other islands, Nauru probably did not have much toxic waste except for old drums of grease and other petroleum products associated with running mine machinery. We learned that Kinza Clodumar, the Nauruan president whose speeches and environmental statements had impressed John and me, had been voted out by Parliament a few months ago. After several hours of conversation we left, knowing this trip was not going to be a typical holiday in the central Pacific.

Weeks after our first day we found that our experiences had destroyed some first impressions and enhanced others. Our efforts to meet with the secretary of external affairs, Angie Itsimaera, who had requested we delay our visit, continued to be unsuccessful, which was unfortunate because governmental sanction of our visit would have quickly opened many doors. As we learned in our first week, some expatriates were reluctant to talk with us until our activities were given government approval, because all foreigners serve at the pleasure of the Nauruan government. One must have a Nauruan parent to acquire citizenship — all others, even those married to Nauruans, have no permanent status. I felt constrained and uneasy about our not having talked with Secretary Itsimaera about our visit, but from the first day Nauruans and many expatriates alike went out of their way to acquaint us with their island home.

Pene, Bruce's host, was exceptionally kind, as well as considerate of our situation. He was a quiet man perhaps in his mid thirties with a typical Nauruan physique — stocky — and a congenial, easygoing personality. I knew him only by what I saw him do, but even without more information, Pene was obviously a pillar of the community. He was a father of three children and, as an environmental officer, held a position of responsibility in the Ministry of Island Development and Industry. He sang in the Congregational Church choir, preached and coordinated the Saturday evening services as a lay preacher at one of three chapels, and was intensely involved in the youth football program. When we showed an interest, Pene took us to his church and up to Topside to hunt noddy birds. Pene seemed always to be there when we needed a ride or some favor. On our first Saturday night he prevailed upon us to go to a first birthday party.

Cars and people were everywhere as we walked from Pene's van across the road and up the balloon- and candle-lined driveway. In front of a modest house a crowd milled about the sloping yard filled with chairs, tables, and blankets. About 60 meters from the house on a flat area a platform stage had been erected. Two lines of tables in the yard, each about 10 meters long, were heaped with food. We found seats at the edge of the yard while five hundred or so people wandered to their spots — something like 5 percent of the country had gathered to celebrate the first birthday of a baby named Lincoln!

Children were laughing and running about, and almost every inch of the yard was filled with humanity. Everyone became quiet as Pastor Willie Star said grace, and Lincoln's parents made a series of statements, all in Nauruan. The guests served themselves while Pene answered our questions about the food we were eating. After about an hour the stage came alive with a series of performances by dancers, singers, and actors. People of every age participated. Although I did not know any of the words, nor did I glean the meanings of the skits and dances, I understood the smiles, could distinguish the jokes from the serious lines, and could even tell when someone had goofed. Then, as if a magic wand had been waved, everywhere children began to collect and pop the hundreds of balloons strung on trees and bushes about the yard. As we departed, I noticed most families carrying plates piled high with food wrapped in foil. In the past, in many traditional cultures, survival of the first year was not taken for granted, but joyously celebrated. The communal obser-vance of Lincoln's first birthday appeared to follow this tradition. His family was clearly honored to have the island celebrate with them, and the gift of food to the community was a token of their thanks.

Each occasion created new opportunities and Mary made the most of them. Among strangers I am shy, but she will talk to just about anybody, an invaluable trait in getting to know Nauru and its inhabitants. On our second Sunday morning, as we waited in the hotel parking lot for a ride to church that never came, Mary saw a couple drive in whom she thought we had met the night before. She waved. The two people in the car looked at each other but gave no sign of recognition. I said to Mary, "We don't know them." Astutely ignoring my statement, she walked across the parking lot and began a conversation with Maria and Mario Brancalion.

Maria, an Australian on a three-year contract, was teaching high school social sciences while struggling to write a social science textbook on Nauruan culture, because none existed, and Mario, an artist, was doing a series of paintings for the Nauruan government. Within minutes we bonded for a host of reasons but foremost was our mutual interest in and concern for Nauru.

On Monday Mario picked us up mid afternoon for a hike on Topside. They lived in one of the houses built prior to independence for the Australian administrators who worked for the British Phosphate Commissioners. Directly behind their house lay areas that had been mined fifty to ninety years ago, which were easily accessible by old min-ing roads. I was excited as we laced our boots and filled our water bottles. The sides of the path were thick with vegetation radiating out to fill the spaces between the pinnacles. Huge yucca plants with four-meter-tall flowering stalks grew abundantly, and half-century-old tomano trees towered above the almost invisible gray hulks of coral. As John and Linda had been, I was impressed with the resilience of nature and her success at reclaiming the moonscapes we had witnessed in the newly mined areas. Heavy rains had preceded the present four-month dry period, so Topside was green with native vegetation. Alien annuals, however, were wilted and dying back. In many areas native ferns and tomano trees were prominent, and in others, these were the only vegetation. In a few of the lusher places I pushed the thin layer of leaf litter aside to reveal fine-to-coarse-grained phosphate mineral and coral debris, not real soil. Nauru has always been a harsh environment for its biota, and mining has made it even harsher.

At Maria's house, no sooner had we removed our boots than the harbor master, Rölf Underdahl, showed up with fish for dinner. Mario's fantastic three-course meal provided the accompaniment to Rölf's humorous tales of twenty-five years of piloting ships in Papua New Guinea and Nauru and to our less humorous commentaries on the yet-unaddressed financial disaster being visited upon the inhabitants of Nauru. Eight or so years ago 1.5 million tons of phosphate were shipped annually from the island, but in subsequent years the tonnage dropped to about half a million, resulting in the NPC's operating at a loss, because for the NPC profits only accrue with tonnages over 600,000 or so. In Nauru's one-product economy, this drop and the subsequent financial losses caused the government and its bank — Nauru's only bank — to run short of money and therefore to be unable to pay their bills and employees.

Maria thinks the Nauruans, like many native peoples, have a disenfranchised middle generation whose members came of age between 1970 and the early 1990s. She explains, "Things are changing now with young people. Some students in my classes are now questioning why things are the way they are. They want to do something to deal with the problems. The old culture has been diluted, and nothing has replaced it. I see hope in these students, but they have no national heroes because they know nothing about their past." She wants them to know something of their past — to know about heroes like Timothy Detudamo, who challenged the Administration in the early 1920s by proposing and then establishing (after time in jail) the first Nauruan-owned business, the Nauru Co-operative Store; who gained higher phosphate royalty rates for the Nauruans during the same time period; and whose wisdom and astute leadership as head chief prior to and during the deportation period of World War II made a very bad situation endurable. Maria's hopeful contribution to the young Nauruans' future is embodied in the textbook she has slaved over after classes and on weekends for most of her time on Nauru.

That night, after our enjoyable time at the Brancalion home, I felt good as I settled into bed with the rumble of surf in the background. We had met many interesting people and were getting a feel for Nauru. On the Sunday we had met Maria and Mario, they drove us to church. After the service, we introduced ourselves to Pastor Willie Star, who invited us to attend the wedding he was about to officiate and then added, "You are invited, of course, to attend the wedding reception at the Menen." We stayed for the church ceremony, but I was uncomfortable about going to the reception. Characteristically, Mary chatted with the photographer, Peter, and soon we were headed for the Menen Hotel with Peter, an uncle of the bride. As we talked, it came out that we wanted to meet the head chief, Paul Aingimea, because his father had been quoted in the *New York Times* article that introduced John and me to Nauru. Like magic, we were at the table of honored guests and family, sitting directly across from Head Chief Aingimea and Pastor Star. Conversation transited smoothly between Nauruan and English, but Pastor Star never spoke in English other than to greet us. Paul was interested in our visit and said we should come to his office at ten in the morning on Tuesday to meet his father.

At eighty-seven, the Reverend James Aingimea, Paul's father, had a slight build and was just over five and a half feet tall. He talked of his life — his experiences as the first Nauruan to go to seminary and to become a minister, his deportation to Truk and, after the Japanese surrender, his role in alerting the U.S. Navy to the Nauruan presence on

Truk, his ministry in Papua New Guinea — but not about Nauru's current situation. Paul was interested in the early literature about Nauru that I had mentioned and asked me to send him copies. He had read the 1997 *Readers' Digest* article and put it in the same class as the 1990 Cousteau video on Nauru: "Not balanced. Focused too much on the negative."

The faxes I received from the secretary of external affairs several days before our departure were in response to a letter I had sent to the Reverend James Aingimea, a Congregational minister, asking for help during our visit. Since we knew no one with contacts on Nauru and Mary's parents are both retired Congregational ministers, we decided to invoke this tenuous connection and to write to him. As it turned out, the Reverend Aingimea had retired, and the letter came to Pastor Star's attention. It didn't look much like church business to him so he gave the letter to the office of the secretary of external affairs. Since the Nauruans have not been well represented by the media, their government is suspicious of all writers and video makers wishing to come to Nauru. I certainly don't blame them, but I also know how important their story is — and it would be most unfortunate to leave it untold.

After church on our third Sunday, Pastor Star invited us to lunch at the Chinese restaurant across from the church. He listened with interest as I told him about the book John and I had written and how his country's story is representative of what is happening on a planetary scale and that we had come to Nauru to see if the Nauruan story could be used as part of an educational video. He told us he would talk with Joseph Cain, director of the Ministry of Island Development and Industry, and suggested we write a letter to Secretary Itsimaera clearly and concisely explaining what we want to do and why. As we left the restaurant, he said, "Come, I want to show you something." We got into his car and he drove several kilometers north, past the phosphate works, and stopped in front of a simple, unimposing one-story chapel with a bell tower. As we stepped out of his car into the heat of the noonday sun, he said, "Before deportation to Truk, Head Chief Timothy Detudamo had many of the young women married. An important distinction, you know. One day on Truk the Japanese commander came to Detudamo and asked for young women to serve tea." Pastor Star gave me a penetrating look with just the hint of a smile in his timeworn face. "Detudamo looked the commander in the eye, ran his finger across his throat as he said, 'Only after you slit my throat.' The commander left without any women. After the war, we built this to honor Detudamo for the many things he had done."

We got back in the car and proceeded to the Menen Hotel. Along the way, without any prompting, he told us that long before Western food and phosphate wealth came, the Nauruans were big people, even obese. "I don't know about diabetes and other diseases in earlier times, but I want to stress that we need to be cautious in our assumptions and inter-pretations," he warned. Although health records indicate that no deaths were attributed to diabetes in the first decades of the twentieth century, Pastor Star's admonition stands. Inferences about another culture should be made carefully and with humility.

Again, on the following Sunday, Pastor Star invited us to lunch. I sensed that he was at ease with us. He recalled his attendance at President Ronald Reagan's inauguration, a discussion in Washington, D.C., about the 200-mile fishing limits, and the Nauruan government's initial invest-ment objective, established in the 1970s, to preserve capital and only spend the interest from investments. He confided that he doesn't really understand why the government is unwilling to talk with us about our video proposal. He went on, "This is my personal opinion. You have worked hard to meet with the government and should just move on." After several long visits with Pastor Star over the almost four-week period, I believed that he was beginning to trust us and that he knew we did not intend to malign his people. Several days later, we were pleased when Secretary Itsimaera met with us and, after a wide-ranging discus-sion, offered her help if we chose to pursue the video project.

Mary is a first-grade teacher and I am a university professor, so it was nat-ural for us to get involved with Nauru's schools. Mary talked about her school and our lives in Troy to every second- and third-grade class at

Yaren Primary School, while I talked with all of Maria's high school classes. We brought slides of our vegetable garden even though we hadn't known that vegetable gardens just aren't found on Nauru. Inspired, one third grader drew Mrs. Mary's garden filled with banana and coconut trees. Reality is what we know.

Kun Te Lee, chief of operations at the Republic of China's Agricultural Technical Mission on Nauru, told us, "Agriculture requires three things: freshwater, fertile arable land, and people to work the land." From the beginning of human habitation on Nauru, supplies of freshwater have been limited, especially in dry periods. Nauru's coastal soils are among the poorest in the world, and the limited quantity of Topside's soil is piled in the center of the island. While Mr. Lee's group has demonstrated the feasibility of growing a number of crops — okra, cucumbers, cabbage, leeks, eggplant, squash, papaya, bananas, and others — Nauruans will have difficulty scaling up his test plots into an island agriculture.

Mario picked us up about 9:30 A.M., and we drove to Maria's school. She greeted us in the parking lot, and we walked to her classroom through open-air walkways with a roof for protection from sun and rain. The front blackboard in her classroom was filled with neatly written material for students to copy, while maps, diagrams — ecosystems, fisheries, atmospheric circulation — and student papers and projects hung on all of the available wall space. I set up the slide projector and tested the projection while Mario hung cloth over the windows to darken the room. Maria introduced me to the first few students who entered, but soon they were coming too fast for individual introductions. The brilliant white, spotless blouses and shirts set off the exuberance in their tan, youthful faces. I am not usually attentive to appearances, but Maria's students stunned me — they were picture-postcard beautiful. The girls smiled and giggled, while the boys were more reserved as we waited for Maria to bring order. My slides guided the talk — world geography, Troy, home, family, garden, climate change, population, biodiversity, economics — while I tried to engage the students with humor and questions. They were very polite and shy. We had a few cases of clear engagement and understanding, but as with most events like this, I couldn't be sure of what had been communicated.

One of Maria's Nauruan colleagues sat in on my talk and was intrigued by what I had said. As we sat and chatted in the staff room between classes, she asked, "What are we to do? When my children ask this, I answer that in a few years we will just have to leave." She wanted to know what gave me any reason to be hopeful for Nauru. I do not remember the details of my response — it is never hopeless, people can identify problems and find solutions, it won't be easy — but I am sure that it was too general to have any meaning within the context of her life on Nauru. Yet, her response to my talk went to the heart of the matter. Is there really hope? Or is hope just an evolutionary concoction in the human brain that has served us well but does not square with the biological and physical reality of an over-exploited planet? Has this marvelous evolutionary adventure on earth created an intelligent species whose success has laid the foundation for its failure?

In contrast to most places we have lived and visited, on Nauru we saw no vagrants, no beggars, no one who was hungry, and no one ever hustled us to buy something. In some very loose way, everybody appears connected to everybody else and people's basic needs are met. They have no tourist industry and absolutely no interest in attracting visitors to their island. In fact, the only industry on the island was the dying NPC — others just don't seem to take root. In town we saw a new, large corrugated metal building with a series of signs across the front that read NAURU'S NO. 1, SOFT DRINK & BOTTLING PLANT, BE NAURUAN, BUY NAURUAN, BACK NAURUAN, ESTABLISHED JULY 1995. What a great idea. Don't import soda, localize the industry. Excited, we went inside to try some Noddy, a soft drink, only to find that the company was not making it anymore, just selling off the stock before going out of business.

Like everywhere else, Nauruans have several sports that garner widespread, enthusiastic support — Australian-rules football, weight lifting, and capturing and taming frigate birds (an ancient sport). The bartender in the Menen Hotel loved Australian-rules football and had a game on the television whenever possible. A high school football team came from Australia for a week of training and two exhibition games. With the recent discovery that Nauruans have real weight-lifting talent, a training center has been built and a sports director from Australia, Paul Coffa, was hired with the hope of making Nauruans competitive against the best weight lifters in the world. In a recent Pacific regional competition Nauruans won 39 gold medals in weight lifting. In order to promote sports in general and Nauruan sports in particular, a substantial sum of money has been spent in establishing Sports Pacific Network, a television station to broadcast sports programs to the central Pacific. Just like in the United States, and in my hometown, Troy, people's minds and hearts are not focused on the issues that brought us to Nauru. They are not talking about biodiversity loss, overpopulation, excessive consumption, or climate change, yet these issues lurk in the shadows of their and our existence and catch the light more frequently now than a decade ago.

Nauru, as a signer of the 1997 agreement the Framework Convention on Climate Change, is a participant in the Pacific Island Climate Change Assistance Program (PICCAP). PICCAP has money for educating a select group of local people about climate change, who are subsequently to educate the rest of their island's inhabitants. Then, as an informed group, the people of each island nation are to plan their response to climate change and ocean level rise. The National Seminar on Climate Change held at the Menen Hotel in the first week of July was part of the PICCAP educational process, and as I contemplated the talks and discussions, I considered Nauru an anomaly. Even if everybody on the island understands the climate change conundrum as well as the speakers, would it make a difference? What are the choices if the sea level does rise significantly when all of the habitable land is only a few meters above current sea level? There is nowhere to go on this island. Yet is Nauru really an anomaly? The likely consequences of significant climate change — dramatic acceleration of the ongoing mass extinction, unpredictable fluctuations in agricultural yields, substantial flooding of coastal areas, increased ranges of parasites and diseases, more violent and extreme weather — would affect all humankind and leave much of the burgeoning human population homeless and without the resources necessary for individual survival and civil order. In a fully populated world, displaced people would have nowhere to go or would fight to the death to acquire space already claimed. Resource and ethnic conflicts of the worst kind — like those we are already seeing in Africa and Eastern Europe — would be commonplace. Certainly it is wise to plan for climate change because it will come even without human influence. At the same time, we are monumentally unwise to force climate change by radically altering the composition of the atmosphere.

I came to experience present-day Nauru and to peer into the future. What I saw and heard, for the most part, confirmed our assessments about Nauru, but a contentious future is closer and far more challenging than John and I had anticipated. The population problem has not even been recognized in any meaningful way. Ironically, in 1919 a British administrator convinced the Nauruans that if their population did not exceed 1,500, they as a people were likely to become extinct, whereas in fact this number was close to, if not above, the carrying capacity of the island before westerners arrived. With a Nauruan population of over 7,000 (in addition to 3,000 foreigners) and a fertility rate of about 5 to 8 children per woman, the Nauruans have one of the faster growing populations in the world.

The financial status of Nauru is not publicly disclosed, nor did we hear it discussed in any overt way among its citizens. No newspapers are routinely published, nor can one access government documents or records in a public library; in fact, the only library we heard of was a small collection of books for pleasure reading maintained by the NPC staff. But the signs of hard financial times were easy to see. Many of the Chinese shops and restaurants had been abandoned, and those that remained open were not very busy. The public transport system no longer existed and many public places were in disrepair. Basic supplies like textbooks and paper were in short supply in the schools. Public announcements on TV stated that government employees would not be paid on time, which confirmed numerous private comments. As part of a chain reaction endemic to the chaotic world economic system, the severe economic woes of a number of Asian countries accelerated the erosion of Nauru's already shaky financial position.

The physical and biological destruction of Topside was certainly expected, but the relevance of this destruction is soon apparent when weak sustainability fails. The remaining ecological productivity of the island is insufficient to feed, clothe, house, and accommodate the current population or, to a lesser degree, a growing population. As long ago as 1945, it was demonstrated that Nauru could not support 5,000 people even with most of Topside intact. When the Allied forces cut the supply lines to Nauru, night soil in 55-gallon drums became the gardens that kept the Nauruans alive — as well as thousands of others — but barely. Today, if supply ships failed to come to Nauru because nothing remained to be traded for the food and materials needed to sustain life, existence would be miserable and people would die, and a severe drought would quickly wreak unimaginable havoc. For a civilization to rely on a weakly sustainable economy is like a tightrope walker performing on a frayed rope without safety nets.

Wes Jackson, co-founder of the Land Institute, wants to set up the ecological books in Matfield Green, a small community in the heart of Kansas. The goal is to have hard data on what comes and goes, and what needs to be done to achieve, or at least to move toward, ecological balance. On one hand, Matfield Green, like most of the rest of the world, is not in ecological balance, but the reality and meaning of the imbalances are hidden because Matfield Green is integrated into the North American continent and the U.S. economic system. On the other hand, because Nauru is ecologically and economically isolated from everywhere else by thousands of kilometers of Pacific Ocean, its ecological books are exposed to all, and all can see that the island's inhabitants are absolutely dependent upon ecological and human productivity from elsewhere. We have attempted to bring this reality to the world's attention and to address the meaning and consequences of those imbalanced books.

However, I believe the Nauruan situation is extremely difficult and complex, because Nauruan culture has been only superficially changed by the world market economy. Nauruans, prior to Western discovery and right up to World War II, continued to live primarily on a diet of coconuts, pandanus, fish, and other native foods. They were, by and large, foragers who subsisted on the biological bounty of their island and its surrounding reef and ocean. All of the necessities of life — water, food, clothing, shelter, human interactions — were readily available and easily acquired in the island's pleasant but warm, humid tropical climate. As in other forager cultures, a steady eight-hour workday was unheard of and silly. Even today the pattern of work for most Nauruans is different from that of market-based, industrialized countries. Instead Nauruan culture has maintained its forager perspective through the past two hundred years. In the three decades since independence Nauruans have merely used money to replace nets, hooks, spears, and hands to hunt and gather from the global, instead of the local, bounty. They have not so much adapted to the market economy as they have fit the market economy into their traditional cultural patterns.

In a future without phosphate, the Nauruans will find their traditional perspective harder and harder to maintain, especially if their attempt to participate in an economy characterized by weak sustainability fails, which appears to be occurring. And, of course, they will fail if their fertility rate continues to double their population every thirty or forty years. So where is the hope? Nauruans are now receiving meaningful negative feedback signals from the market economy. They are at a crossroads as they were in 1968 — when the market economy gave no negative feedback signals — but without the phosphate they had then and the biological integrity they have extinguished since that time. If they are to maintain their culture on Nauru, they will have to create long-term approaches that address the fundamental necessity of living within their now severely impoverished physical and biological environment, as well as within their financial means.

As in 1968, the Nauruans again have a unique opportunity to be a role model for the rest of us. With only seven thousand citizens, it is possible for every Nauruan to have a hand in creating Nauruan approaches and solutions for Nauruan problems. Perhaps they might create a consensus-based pattern of decision making — a possibility with such a small population. They could establish a public forum to discuss the myriad challenges associated with creating enduring habitation, including population policy, the purpose of education, and what Nauruan children and adults need to learn in order that each might make a contribution to the success of the group's long-term goals. If the Nauruans can re-create a sustainable pattern of habitation on Nauru, then the rest of us may gain hope for humankind. To reestablish a sustainable culture will not be easy for the Nauruans; however, the alternatives are not solutions but rather capitulations to a failed economic system.

Since my return from Nauru, John and I have come to appreciate more than ever that Nauru's story is, in fact, a parable for the earth itself. Most people in the industrialized world sing, dance, party, get excited about and spend extravagantly on sports and other forms of entertainment, enjoy food, delight in babies and children, take passionate pride in their own accomplishments, consider their worldview correct, think technology will solve their problems, and assume human superiority over and separateness from the rest of creation. These behaviors, attitudes, and emotions are grounded in our cultural myths and beliefs, which some may consider affirmed by the phenomenal achievements we witness every day: instant global communication, organ transplants, eradication of diseases, space travel and exploration, computer technology, genetic engineering, enormous diversity of foods, wonder drugs, travel everywhere, and ever-increasing life expectancy, to name but a few.

In other words, our scientific technological economic system has delivered the goods! Conventional wisdom tells us, "If it ain't broke, don't fix it." However, now that the entire earth and its biodiversity are being overexploited, do Nauru and innumerable other examples tell us that our economic system is, in fact, dysfunctional? Does enduring habitation in a world overflowing with humans and impoverished by humanity's current pattern of habitation demand rethinking our relationships with the rest of creation and with each other? We think it does and join those who see monumental trouble ahead if we continue on our current path. Unfortunately, our culture's successes have resulted in overwhelming inertia, while past cultural failures are hard to accept as relevant and fundamental changes are even more difficult to implement. Like the Nauruans, who faced a critical turning point in 1968, the world economic culture has chosen a path of nonsustainability and certain destruction; but like the people of Tikopia, perhaps we can change direction. However, without unprecedented and rapid cultural change, we believe human civilization, as we know it, will collapse — either with excruciating slowness over centuries or with cataclysmic suddenness over decades — and the path down is sure to be unpleasant. Yet we, as a global aggregate of humans, certainly do have the knowledge and the resources — biological and otherwise — to achieve enduring habitation.

Notes

Prelude

3 "A Pacific Island Nation Is Stripped of Everything," *New York Times* (Internet service), December 10, 1995.

9 Paul Ehrlich and Anne Ehrlich, *The Betrayal of Science and Reason* (Washington, D.C.: Island Press, 1996). The review of the Ehrlichs' book is by Daniel Sarewitz, "Science and Sensibility," *Science* 274 (1996): 198.

Chapter One. A Pleasant Island

13 The major books about Nauru are by William Fabricus, *Nauru* (Canberra: Australian National University Press, 1992), originally published in 1895 and translated by Dymphna Clark and Stewart Firth; Albert Ellis, *Ocean Island and Nauru: Their Story* (Sydney: Angus and Robertson LTD, 1935); Nancy Viviani, *Nauru: Phosphate and Political Progress* (Canberra: Australian National University Press, 1970); Maslyn Williams and Barrie Macdonald, *The Phosphateers* (Melbourne: Melbourne University Press, 1985); Barrie Macdonald, *In Pursuit of the Sacred Trust. Trusteeship and Independence in Nauru* (Wellington, NZ: New Zealand Institute of International Affairs, Occasional Paper No. 3, 1988); Christopher Weeramantry, *Nauru: Environmental Damage under International Trusteeship* (Melbourne: Oxford University

Press, 1992); and Jemima Garrett, *Island Exiles* (Sydney: ABC Books, 1996).

13 The major articles on Nauru prior to independence are Rosamond Dobson Rhone, "Nauru, The Richest Island in the South Seas," *National Geographic Magazine* 40 (1921): 549–89; Camilla H. Wedgwood, "Report on Research Work on Nauru Island, Central Pacific (part one)," *Oceania* 6 (1936a): 359–94; Camilla H. Wedgwood, "Report on Research Work on Nauru Island, Central Pacific (part two)," *Oceania* 7 (1936b): 1–33; Ernest Stephen, "Notes on Nauru," *Oceania* 7 (1936): 34–63.

15–17 An account of pagan, Hebrew, and Christian myths is given in the important and influential book by Arthur O. Lovejoy, *The Great Chain of Being* (Cambridge: Harvard University Press, 1936). See also Morris Berman, *The Reenchantment of the World* (New York: Bantam Books, 1984).

17–18 For a lively account of the origin and influence of the Enlightenment see chapters 2 and 3 in Edward O. Wilson, *Consilience* (New York: Knopf, 1998). The life and thought of Francis Bacon is documented by James Stephens in *Francis Bacon and the Style of Science* (Chicago: University of Chicago Press, 1975). See also Carolyn Merchant, *The Death of Nature: Women, Ecology, and the Scientific Revolution* (San Francisco: Harper and Row, 1980).

18 Nauruan myths including the creation story come from Roslyn Poignant, *Oceanic Mythology — the Myths of Polynesia, Micronesia, Melanesia, and Australia* (London: Paul Hamlyn, 1967), 70–82; *Ninth Annual Report of the Nauru Mission* (missionaries Rev. Ph. A. Delaporte, Mrs. Salome Delaporte, Miss Maria Linke), published for the American Board of Commissioners for Foreign Missions by the Nauru Mission Press, Nauru, Marshall Islands (1910), 31. The account of the loss of myths is from Wedgwood (1936a and 1936b), and the account of sexual practices on Nauru is from Viviani (1970). For further details about language and race in Polynesia, see Wedgwood (1936a), 368–77.

21 The notion among Nauruans that fatness is beautiful is from Stephen (1936), 41, 46.

21–22 Discussion of class structure is from Wedgwood (1936b), 1–4.

21–23   The description of marriage customs is from Wedgwood (1936a), 384–385.

23   Patterns of giving to children are described by Wedgwood (1936b), p. 15.

23–24   Inheritance rights are from Wedgwood (1936b), 20–24.

24   The account of fish raising in Buada Lagoon is found in Wedgwood (1936a), 367; Wedgwood (1936b), 11–14; and Viviani (1970), 6.

24–26   The Nauruan story of the loss and return of the coconut tree is from the *Ninth Annual Report of the Nauru Mission* (1910), 31; the uses of the coconut tree are found in Rhone (1921), 575–79.

24–27   The uses of coconut and pandanus trees and other native plants and animals of Nauru are taken from Rhone (1921), 576–80; and Wedgwood (1936b), 8–9.

Chapter Two. Progress Comes to Nauru

29   Discussion of Ferdinand Magellan's trip is from Simon Winchester, "After Dire Straits, an Agonizing Haul across the Pacific," *Smithsonian* 22 (April 1991): 84–95.

29–30   Accounts of the *Hunter* are given by Albert Ellis, *Ocean Island and Nauru: Their Story* (Sydney: Angus and Robertson LTD, 1935), 29; and Nancy Viviani, *Nauru: Phosphate and Political Progress* (Canberra: Australian National University Press, 1970), 9–10.

30–32   Beachcombing on Nauru is described by Ellis (1935), 29–39; H. E. Maude, "Beachcombers and Castaways," *Journal of the Polynesian Society* 73 (1964): 245–93; and Viviani (1970), 10–11.

33   The account of sour toddy is from William Fabricus, *Nauru,* trans. Dymphna Clark and Stewart Firth (1895; reprint, Canberra: Australian National University Press, 1992), 218–22; and Ellis (1935), 37–38.

34   Civil strife quotation is from Ellis (1935), 35.

35–39   The account of the German occupation of Nauru is from Fabricus (1895); Ellis (1935); and Viviani (1970).

36   Many books have been written about Charles Darwin and evolution. We cite four: Alan Morehead, *Darwin and the Beagle* (New York:

Harper and Row, 1969); Stephen Jay Gould, *Wonderful Life* (New York: W. W. Norton, 1989); Daniel Dennett, *Darwin's Dangerous Idea* (New York: Touchstone, 1995); and Niles Eldredge, *Reinventing Darwin* (New York: John Wiley and Sons, 1995).

39   The lack of disease among Nauruans is described by Camilla H. Wedgwood, "Report on Research Work on Nauru Island, Central Pacific (part one)," *Oceania* 6 (1936a): 368. For the origins and history of human diseases, see Clive Ponting, *A Green History of the World* (New York: Penguin Books, 1991); Jared Diamond, *Guns, Germs, and Steel* (New York: Norton, 1997); and William H. McNeill, *Plagues and Peoples* (New York: Anchor Books, 1998).

39–40   For a full account of how phosphate was discovered on Nauru, see Ellis (1935); and Maslyn Williams and Barrie Macdonald, *The Phosphateers* (Melbourne: Melbourne University Press, 1985).

41   Albert Ellis is quoted in Williams and Macdonald (1985), 39.

41   Details of mining agreements on Banaba and Nauru are from Viviani (1970), 29–31.

42–43   An account of the zealousness of the missionaries is found in Mrs. Philip A. Delaporte, "The Men and Women of Old Nauru," *The Mid Pacific* 19 (1920): 153–56; and Rosamond Dobson Rhone, "Nauru, The Richest Island in the South Seas," *National Geographic Magazine* 40 (1921): 581–83.

44   The Nauru Island Agreement of 1919 is reproduced in Christopher Weeramantry, *Nauru: Environmental Damage under International Trusteeship* (Melbourne: Oxford University Press, 1992), 375–78.

44   An informative account of life on Nauru in the early twentieth century is given by Rhone (1921).

44   Accounts of the Japanese occupation are given in Viviani (1970), chapter 5; Williams and Macdonald (1985), chapter 34; Weeramantry (1992), 411; and Jemima Garrett, *Island Exiles* (Sydney: ABC Books, 1996).

45   The dollar values for phosphate revenues and allocations to administration and to the Nauruans can be found in Viviani (1970) and Weeramantry (1992).

45–47   A detailed discussion of Nauruan independence and the events leading up to it is given by Viviani (1970); Barrie Macdonald, *In Pursuit of the Sacred Trust. Trusteeship and Independence in Nauru* (Wellington, NZ: New Zealand Institute of International Affairs, Occasional Paper No. 3, 1988); and Weeramantry (1992).

46 Value of "Compact of Settlement" taken from *Mining Journal* (London), 321, no. 8240 (September 3, 1993): 158–59.

47 Treatment of Banabans from Fred Pearce, "Pity the Poor Banabans," *New Scientist* (March 22, 1997): 48.

47–51 Discussions and data on Nauru after independence can be found in the following: Mike Holmes, "This Is the World's Richest Nation — All of It!" *National Geographic* (September 1976): 344–53; Hamish McDonald, "Wanting Their Cake Now," *Far Eastern Economic Review* (June 12, 1986): 127; Macdonald (1988), 59–69; M. Malik, "Ruined Republic," *Far Eastern Economic Review* (June 23–24, 1989); A. Anghie, "The Heart of My Home: Colonialism, Environmental Damage, and the Nauru Case," *Harvard International Law Journal* 34 (1993): 445–506; "A Pacific Island Nation Is Stripped of Everything," *New York Times* (Internet service), December 10, 1995; P. A. Van Atta, "Paradise Squandered," *Reader's Digest* (May 1997): 87–91.

49 Data and an analysis of lifestyle change on Nauru are given in Helen J. Rubinstein and Paul Zimmet, *Phosphate, Wealth and Health in Nauru: A Study of Lifestyle Change* (Gundaroo, NSW, Australia: Brolga Press, 1993).

49 Life expectancy on Nauru is from R. Taylor and K. Thoma, "Mortality Patterns in the Modernized Pacific Island Nation of Nauru," *American Journal of Public Health* 75 (1985): 149–55.

49 For information on changing eating habits of Pacific islanders, see R. R. Thaman, "Deterioration of Traditional Food Systems, Increasing Malnutrition and Food Dependency in the Pacific Islands," *Journal of Food and Nutrition* 39 (1982): 109–21.

49–50 For a description of biodiversity loss and plant succession on Nauru, see H. I. Manner, R. R. Thaman, and D. C. Hassall, "Phosphate-Mining Induced Vegetation Changes on Nauru Island," *Ecology* 65 (1984): 1454–65; H. I. Manner, R. R. Thaman, and D. C. Hassall, "Plant Succession after Phosphate Mining on Nauru," *Australian Geographer* 17

(1985): 185–95; H. I. Manner and R. J. Morrison, "Changes in Soil Carbon and Nitrogen after Mining: A Temporal Sequence (Chronosequence) of Soil Carbon and Nitrogen Development after Phosphate Mining on Nauru Island," *Pacific Science* 4 (1991): 400–404; Randolph R. Thaman, "Vegetation of Nauru and the Gilbert Islands: Case Studies of Poverty, Degradation, Disturbance, and Displacement," *Pacific Science* 46 (1992): 128–58.

Chapter Three. Nauru's Shadow

52 The quotation by Kinza Clodumar is from P. A. Van Atta, "Paradise Squandered," *Reader's Digest* (May 1997): 88.

52 The Wes Jackson quotation is from his book *Altars of Unhewn Stone* (San Francisco: North Point Press, 1987), 9.

52 For an account of the effects of El Niño and La Niña southern oscillation on human cultures in the Pacific, see Tim Flannery, *The Future Eaters: An Ecological History of the Australian Lands and People* (Port Melbourne: Reed Books, 1994).

54 For the classic account of island biogeography, see Robert McArthur and Edward O. Wilson, *The Theory of Island Biogeography* (Princeton: Princeton University Press, 1967).

54 An account of the effects of human settlement of the Pacific islands is given by Andrew Mitchell, *A Fragile Paradise* (London: Fontana/Collins, 1989); and Patrick Kirch and Terry Hunt, eds., *Historical Ecology of the Pacific Islands* (New Haven: Yale University Press, 1997).

54–56 Discussions of plant diversity and species loss on Nauru and comparisons with other islands are given by H. I. Manner, R. R. Thaman, and D. C. Hassall, "Phosphate-Mining Induced Vegetation Changes on Nauru Island," *Ecology* 65 (1984): 1454–65; H. Manner, R. Thaman, and D. Hassall, "Plant Succession after Phosphate Mining on Nauru," *Australian Geographer* 16 (1985): 185–95; J-F. Dupon. "Pacific Phosphate Island Environments versus the Mining Industry: An Unequal Struggle," Environmental Case Studies, South Pacific Study 4, South Pacific Regional Environment Programme (New Caledonia: South Pacific Commission, 1989); H. Manner and A. J. Morrison, "A Temporal Sequence (Chronosequence) of Soil Carbon and Nitrogen Development after Phosphate Mining on Nauru," *Pacific Science* 45 (1991): 400–404; R. R. Thaman, "Vegetation of Nauru and the Gilbert Islands: Case Studies of Poverty, Degradation, Disturbance, and Displacement," *Pacific Science* 46 (1992): 128–58.

55   The ecological impact of alien species is detailed by Harold Mooney and James A. Drake, eds., *Ecology of Biological Invasions in North America and Hawaii* (New York: Springer, 1986); David Quammen, *The Song of the Dodo* (New York: Touchstone, 1996); John Travis, "Invader Threatens Black, Azov Seas," *Science* 262 (1993): 1366–67; Virginia Morell, "Australian Pest Control by Virus Causes Concern," *Science* 261 (1993): 683–84; Charles C. Mann, "Fire Ants Parlay Their Queens into a Threat to Biodiversity," *Science* 263 (1993): 1560–61; and Gábor L. Lövei, "Global Change through Invasion," *Nature* 388 (1997): 627–28.

56   The song "Heart of My Home" is from Christopher Weeramantry, *Nauru: Environmental Damage under International Trusteeship* (Melbourne: Oxford University Press, 1992), 30.

57–59   Accounts of biodiversity loss and the functions and materials of ecosystems are given by Edward O. Wilson, *The Diversity of Life* (Cambridge: Harvard University Press, 1992); Peter Ward, *The End of Evolution* (New York: Bantam Books, 1994); Andrew Dobson, *Conservation and Biodiversity* (New York: W. H. Freeman, 1996); Niles Eldredge, *Life in the Balance* (Princeton: Princeton University Press, 1998); and Richard Leaky and Richard Lewin, *The Sixth Extinction* (New York: Doubleday, 1995).

57–58   The story of the passenger pigeon is in A. Schorger, *The Passenger Pigeon* (Norman: University of Oklahoma Press, 1973).

58   The decrease in number of American songbirds is discussed in John Terborgh, "Why American Songbirds Are Vanishing," *Scientific American* 266 (May 1992): 98–104.

58   The fate of the buffalo is detailed by F. Roe, *The North American Buffalo,* 2d ed. (Toronto: University of Toronto Press, 1970); David Dary, *The Buffalo Book* (Columbus: Swallow Press/Ohio University Press, 1989); and Ernest Callenbach, *Bring back the Buffalo* (Washington, D.C.: Island Press, 1996).

58–59   Accounts of the magnitude of biodiversity loss are given in E. O. Wilson, ed., *Biodiversity* (Washington, D.C.: National Academy Press, 1988); Wilson (1992); S. Pimm et al., "The Future of Biodiversity," *Science* 269 (June 21, 1995): 347–50; and Beverly Peterson Stearns and Stephen C. Stearns, *Watching from the Edge of Extinction* (New Haven: Yale University Press, 1999). See also the February 1999 issue of *National Geographic,* titled "Biodiversity."

59–62   Overpopulation is discussed by Werner Fornos, *Gaining People, Losing Ground* (Ephrata, Penn.: Science Press, 1987); Lindsey Grant, *Elephants in the Volkswagen* (San Francisco: W. H. Freeman, 1992); and Joel E. Cohen, *How Many People Can the Earth Support?* (New York: Norton, 1995). See the population size calculations in John Gowdy and Carl McDaniel, "One World, One Experiment: Addressing the Biodiversity-Economics Conflict," *Ecological Economics* 15 (1995): 181–92.

62   Human appropriation of the products of available photosynthesis is calculated by P. M. Vitousek et al., "Human Appropriation of the Products of Photosynthesis: Nearly 40% of Potential Terrestrial Net Primary Productivity Is Used Directly, Coopted, or Foregone Because of Human Activity," *BioScience* 36 (1986): 368–73.

63   We used two methods to calculate the amount of net land photosynthetic product used by humans 10,000 years ago.

First, in 1986, 5 billion humans were using about 40 percent of the net land photosynthetic product; thus, the estimated 4 million people on earth 10,000 years ago (Clive Ponting, *A Green History of the World*, New York: Penguin Books, 1991) would have used about 0.04 percent if they had lived as we do, but they didn't. An approximation of the difference in use of land photosynthesis (direct and indirect) is obtained by comparing the energy used now and 10,000 years ago (per capita increase mostly from burning fossil fuels). Humans today use at least 20 times the energy per capita than do hunter-gatherers (Earl Cook, "The Flow of Energy in an Industrial Society," *Scientific American* 224 [September 1971]: 134–44). Thus, humans used about 0.002 percent of net land photosynthetic product 10,000 years ago.

Second, the total net world photosynthetic product is about 3.0×10^{20} calories/year [$(40 \times 10^{12}$ joules/second) $\times$ (1 calorie/4.2 joules) $\times$ $(3.2 \times 10^7$ seconds/year)] (Jack J. Kraushaar and Robert A. Ristinen, *Energy and Problems of a Technological Society*, 2d ed. [New York: John Wiley, 1993]). Assume the average person eats 2,500 kilocalories/day, or 9.1 × 10⁵ kilocalories/year (2,500 kilocalories/day × 365 days); four million people would use 3.6 × 10¹² kilocalories/year (9.1 × 10⁵ kilocalories/year/person × 4 × 10⁶ persons); four million people would eat about 0.0012 percent of the net world photosynthetic product [(3.6 × 10¹² kilocalories/year) ÷ (3.0 × 10¹⁷ kilocalories/year) × 100]. About half of world photosynthesis takes place in the oceans; thus, humans would use about 0.0024 percent for food. If we assume fires for cooking and heating consumed an equivalent amount of energy, humans used about 0.005 percent of the net land photosynthetic product 10,000 years ago.

63   For a wonderful account of the prairie ecology, economy and culture, see William Least-Heat Moon, *PrairyErth* (Boston: Houghton Mifflin, 1991).

63–64   Industrial agriculture and its consequences are discussed in Wes Jackson, *New Roots for Agriculture* (San Francisco: Friends of the Earth, 1980); Wes Jackson, Wendell Berry, and Bruce Colman, eds., *Meeting the Expectations of the Land* (San Francisco: North Point Press, 1984); William E. Riebsame, "The United States Great Plains," in *The Earth as Transformed by Human Action*, ed. B. L. Turner II et al. (Cambridge: Cambridge University Press, 1990), 561–75; Judith D. Soule and Jon K. Piper, *Farming in Nature's Image* (Washington, D.C.: Island Press, 1992); Alan Wild, *Soils and the Environment* (Cambridge: Cambridge University Press, 1993); Michael H. Glantz, *Drought Follows the Plow* (Cambridge: Cambridge University Press, 1994); and Gary Gardner, "Shrinking Fields: Cropland Loss in a World of Eight Billion," Worldwatch Paper 131 (Washington, D.C.: Worldwatch Institute, 1996).

63   Erosion and soil formation rates: David Pimentel et al., "Environmental and Economic Costs of Soil Erosion and Conservation Benefits," *Science* 267 (1995): 1117–23.

64–65   Land requirements for the Dutch population at current lifestyle are given in Mathis Wackernagal and William Rees, *Our Ecological Footprint* (Gabriola Island, B.C.: New Society Publishers, 1996).

65   Human population is discussed by Thomas Malthus, Julian Huxley, and Frederick Osborn, *Three Essays on Population* (New York: New American Library, Mentor Book, 1960); Roy Greep, ed., *Human Fer-*

tility and Population Problems (Cambridge, Mass.: Schenkman Publishing Co., 1963); Paul Ehrlich and Anne Ehrlich, *The Population Explosion* (New York: Touchstone, 1990); Cohen (1995); and Joel Cohen, "Population Growth and Earth's Human Carrying Capacity," *Science* 269 (1995): 341–46.

66–69   Earth's climate and climate change: Stephen Schneider, *Global Warming: Are We Entering the Greenhouse Century?* (San Francisco: Sierra Club Books, 1989); John Houghton, *Global Warming: The Complete Briefing* (Cambridge: Cambridge University Press, 1997); Edward Bryant, *Climate Process & Change* (Cambridge: Cambridge University Press, 1997); Ross Gelbspan, *The Heat Is ON* (New York: Addison-Wesley Publishing Company, 1997).

67   The danger posed to low-lying Pacific islands by sea level rise due to global warming is from Nicholas Kristof, "For Pacific Islanders, Global Warming Is No Idle Threat," *New York Times* (Internet service), March 2, 1997.

68–69   Ocean current reversal is discussed by Wallace S. Broecker, "Thermohaline Circulation, the Achilles Heel of Our Climate System: Will Man-Made CO2 Upset the Current Balance?" *Science* 278 (1997): 1582–88; and William Calvin, "The Great Climate Flip-flop," *Atlantic Monthly* (January 1998): 47–64.

Chapter Four. Living the Myths

70   The Kliuchesky quotation is in Robert Heilbroner, *Twenty-First Century Capitalism* (New York: W. W. Norton, 1994), 13.

70   The Brundtland Commission quotation is from the World Commission on Environment and Development, *Our Common Future* (Cambridge: Oxford University Press, 1987), 114–15.

70–71   For an account of early humans, see Jared Diamond, *The Third Chimpanzee* (New York: HarperCollins, 1992); and Rick Potts, *Humanity's Descent* (New York: William Morrow, 1996). Information about our early human ancestors is changing so fast it is impossible to have up-to-date information in a book. During the past decade, numerous findings have increased our appreciation for the complexity of the cultures of early humans.

71–73   Discussions of genetics and human behavior can be found in any introductory biology textbook. See, for example Peter H. Raven and
George B. Johnson, *Biology,* 5th ed. (Boston: WCB McGraw-Hill,
1999); and Teresa Audesirk and Gerald Audesirk, *Biology: Life on
Earth,* 4th ed. (Upper Saddle River, N.J.: Prentice-Hall, 1996).

Detailed discussions of genetics, behavior, and culture are found in
Edward O. Wilson, *Sociobiology: The New Synthesis* (Cambridge: Harvard University Press, Belknap Press, 1976); Edward O. Wilson, *On
Human Nature* (Cambridge: Harvard University Press, Belknap Press,
1978); Constance Holden, "Reunited Twins: More Than Faces Are
Familiar," *Science* 80 (1980): 54–59; "Genes and Behavior," A Special
Report, *Science* 264 (1994): 1686–739; Edward O. Wilson, *Consilience*
(New York: Knopf, 1998); Robert Plomin and Jon C. DeFries, "The
Genetics of Cognitive Abilities and Disabilities," *Scientific American*
(May 1998): 62–69; David S. Wilson, "Human Groups as Units of
Selection," *Science* 276 (1997): 1816–17; and C. Boehm, "Impact of the
Human Egalitarian Syndrome on Darwinian Selection Mechanics,"
American Naturalist 15 (1997): S100–21.

74–77   Information about Australian aborigines can be found in D. Bates, *The
Native Tribes of Western Australia* (Canberra: National Library of Australia, 1985); Ronald M. Berndt and Catherine H. Berndt, *The World of
the First Australians* (Canberra: Aboriginal Studies Press, 1988); M. G.
Bicchieri, *Hunters and Gatherers Today* (Prospect Heights, Ill.: Waveland Press, 1988); Tony Dingle, *Aboriginal Economy* (Victoria, Australia: Penguin Books, 1988); Tim Flannery, *The Future Eaters: An Ecological History of the Australian Lands and People* (Port Melbourne:
Reed Books, 1995); and J. Gowdy, ed., *Limited Wants, Unlimited Means:
A Hunter-Gatherer Reader on Economics and the Environment* (Washington, D.C.: Island Press, 1998).

74–75   Sources for the cultural and environmental history of Australia are:
Robert Hughes, *The Fatal Shore: The Epic of Australia's Founding* (New
York: Vintage Books, 1988); and John Rickard, *Australia: A Cultural
History* (Essex, U.K.: Longman Group UK Limited, 1988).

77–82   Accounts of the !Kung are found in Richard B. Lee, "What Hunters
Do for a Living, or, How to Make Out on Scarce Resources," in *Man
the Hunter*, ed. R. Lee and I. Devore (New York: Aldine de Gruyter,

1968) (also in Gowdy [1998]); Lorna Marshall, "Sharing, Talking, and Giving: Relief of Social Tensions among the !Kung," in *Kalahari Hunter-Gatherers*, ed. R. Lee and I. Devore (Cambridge: Harvard University Press, 1976) (also in Gowdy [1998]); John Yellen, "The Transformation of the Kalahari !Kung," *Scientific American* (April 1990): 96–105 (also in Gowdy [1998]); Richard B. Lee, *The Dobe Ju/'hoansi*, 2d ed. (New York: Harcourt Brace, 1993); and David Goodman, "Africa's Oldest Survivors," *World Monitor* (April 1993): 38–44.

79–80   Patterns of sharing and egalitarianism have been documented by Colin Turnbull, *The Forest People* (New York: Simon and Schuster, 1962); James Woodburn, "Egalitarian Societies," *Man* 17 (1982): 431–51; and Farley Mowat, *The People of the Deer* (New York: Bantam Books, 1985).

82–88   Information on Rapa Nui can be found in Peter Bahn and John Flenley, *Easter Island, Earth Island* (London: Thames and Hudson, 1992); Jo Anne van Tilberg, *Easter Island: Archaeology, Ecology, and Culture* (Washington, D.C.: Smithsonian Institute Press, 1994); Jared Diamond, "Easter's End," *Discover Magazine* (August 1995): 63–68; and James Brander and Scott Taylor, "The Simple Economics of Easter Island: A Ricardo-Malthus Model of Renewable Resource Use," *American Economic Review* 88 (1998): 119–38.

88–90   Accounts of the Greenland Norse are found in Kirsten Seaver, *The Frozen Echo* (Stanford: Stanford University Press, 1996); and Heather Pringle, "Death in Norse Greenland," *Science* 275 (1997): 924–26.

90–94   Information about Ladakh is found in Helena Norberg-Hodge, *Ancient Futures* (San Francisco: Sierra Club Books, 1991).

Chapter Five. Science as Story

95   The quotation is in Niles Eldredge, *Dominion* (Berkeley: University of California Press, 1977), xiv–xv.

95–96   Accounts of the overshoot and collapse of past societies are given by M. Tainter, *The Collapse of Complex Societies* (Cambridge: Cambridge University Press, 1989); and Clive Ponting, *A Green History of the World* (New York: Penguin Books, 1991).

98 Height and life span of Europeans is given in Marvin Harris, *Cannibals and Kings* (New York: Random House, 1977).

98–99 Numerous articles and books have documented the environmental consequences of human activities, and many of these are listed above. One of the best sources of accurate and precise information about these consequences can be found in the publications of the Worldwatch Institute, 1776 Massachusetts Ave., N.W., Washington, D.C. 20036: an annual publication beginning in 1984 titled "State of the World"; an annual publication beginning in 1992 titled "Vital Signs"; Worldwatch Papers; a series of special reports, each focusing on a specific topic; *Worldwatch Magazine;* and periodic books. The other excellent source of this information is any material published by the World Resources Institute, 1709 New York Avenue, N.W., Washington, D.C. 20006, of which the biennial publication *World Resources* is the most informative. A discussion about these data and the misinformation surrounding the issues is given by Paul Ehrlich and Anne Ehrlich, *The Betrayal of Science and Reason: How Anti-Environmental Rhetoric Threatens Our Future* (Washington, D.C.: Island Press, 1996).

99 An accessible presentation of the potential problems associated with exotic chemicals is given in Theo Colborn, Dianne Dumanoski, and John Peterson Myers, *Our Stolen Future* (New York: Penguin Group, 1996).

99–104 The basic science story is found in introductory college biology or geology textbooks. See, for example, Peter H. Raven and George B. Johnson, *Biology,* 5th ed. (Boston: WCB McGraw-Hill, 1999); Teresa Audesirk and Gerald Audesirk, *Biology: Life on Earth,* 4th ed. (Upper Saddle River, N.J.: Prentice-Hall, 1996); and Frank Press and Raymond Siever, *Understanding Earth* (New York: W. H. Freeman, 1994). More general works on this topic include Thomas Berry, *The Dream of the Earth* (San Francisco: Sierra Books, 1988); Stephen Jay Gould, gen. ed., *The Book of Life* (New York: W. W. Norton, 1995); and R. Fortney, *Life: A Natural History of the First Four Billion Years of Life on Earth* (New York: Knopf, 1998).

104–105 Accounts of early humans are given by Clive Gamble, *Timewalkers: The Prehistory of Global Colonization* (Cambridge: Harvard University Press, 1993); and Richard Potts, *Humanity's Descent: The Conse-quences of Ecological Instability* (New York: William Morrow, 1996).

105 Although settled communities and agriculture appeared about the same time, the relationship between the two is still in question, as discussed by Michael Balter, "Why Settle Down? The Mystery of Communities," *Science* 282 (1998): 1442–45. The relations among agriculture, domestication and settled life across the globe are discussed in Heather Pringle, "The Slow Birth of Agriculture," *Science* 282 (1998): 1446–50.

105 An account of the transition to agriculture is given by Douglas Price and Anne Gebauer, eds., *Last Hunters, First Farmers* (Santa Fe, N.M.: Sar Press, 1995).

106 The politics and social structure of the scientific community are introduced in H. Collins and T. Pinch, *The Golem: What Everyone Should Know about Science* (New York: Cambridge University Press, 1993).

107–108 Edward O. Wilson's autobiography, *Naturalist* (Washington, D.C.: Island Press, 1994) gives an excellent account of the process of scientific discovery.

Chapter Six. To Love a Cockroach

109 The Peter Raven quotation is from his lecture titled "What Is Biological Diversity and Why Is It Important to Us?" reprinted in the June 1995 issue of *Environmental Review* (Internet service).

109 Many have written about the biological connections we discuss. A seminal work is Aldo Leopold's *A Sand County Almanac and Sketches Here and There* (Oxford: Oxford University Press, 1949). For discussions of the materials and functions of biodiversity, see Gretchen Daily, *Nature's Services* (Washington, D.C.: Island Press, 1997); and Yvonne Baskin, *The Work of Nature: How the Diversity of Life Sustains Us* (Washington, D.C.: Island Press, 1997).

112–113 Spiritual and health needs from biodiversity are documented by Edward O. Wilson, *Biophilia* (Cambridge: Harvard University Press, Belknap Press, 1984); and S. Kellert and E. O. Wilson, eds., *The Biophilia Hypothesis* (Washington, D.C.: Island Press, 1993).

112–113   Information about Biosphere 2 taken from Baskin (1997).

114–123   Discussions of extinctions are given by E. O. Wilson, *The Diversity of Life* (Cambridge: Harvard University Press, 1992); S. L. Pimm, *The Balance of Nature* (Chicago: University of Chicago Press, 1994); and David Quammen, *The Song of the Dodo* (New York: Simon and Schuster, 1996).

    Assessments of biodiversity loss are given by Peter Ward, *The End of Evolution: A Journey in Search of Clues to the Third Mass Extinction Facing Planet Earth* (New York: Bantam Books, 1994); Stuart Pimm et al., "The Future of Biodiversity," *Science* 269 (1995): 347–50; R. T. Watson et al., *Global Biodiversity Assessment: Summary for Policy-Makers* (Cambridge: Cambridge University Press, 1995); and Niles Eldredge, *Life in the Balance* (Princeton: Princeton University Press, 1998).

118   Reductions in size of ecosystems in the United States given in Reed F. Noss, Edward T. LaRoe III, and J. Michael Scott, *Endangered Ecosystems of the United States: A Preliminary Assessment of Loss and Degradation* (Washington, D.C.: U.S. Department of the Interior, National Biological Service, 1995).

119   Documentation of endangered species is given by Jonathan Baille and Brian Groombridge, *1996 IUNC Red List of Threatened Animals* (Cambridge: IUCN; Washington, D.C.: Conservation International, 1996); the Nature Conservancy's 1996 study of 20,481 species native to the United States was reported in the *New York Times,* January 2, 1996; and a listing and discussion of threatened plants in the world appears in the *1997 IUNC Red List of Threatened Plants* (Washington, D.C.: Island Press, 1997).

121–123   Ecological concepts are found in Robert E. Ricklefs, *Ecology*, 3d ed. (New York: W. H. Freeman, 1990); Eugene P. Odum, *Ecology: Our Endangered Life Support Systems,* 2d ed. (Sunderland, Mass.: Sinauer Associates, 1993); and Pimm (1994).

124–126   Four ecosystem stories are from Baskin (1997).

125   Problems of increased ecosystem nitrogen are highlighted in Anne Simon Moffat, "Global Nitrogen Overload Problem Grows Global," *Science* 279 (1998): 988–89.

126   Easter Island references are Peter Bahn and John Flenley, *Easter Island,*

Earth Island (London: Thames and Hudson, 1992); and Jo Anne van Tilburg, *Easter Island: Archaeology, Ecology, and Culture* (Washington, D.C.: Smithsonian Institute Press, 1994).

127 The profound dangers of exotic chemicals were first definitively presented in Rachel Carson, *Silent Spring* (New York: Houghton Mifflin, 1962).

Chapter Seven. The Market: Master or Servant?

131 The epigraph attributed to Nicholas Georgescu-Roegen is from his book *Energy and Economic Myths* (San Francisco: Pergamon Press, 1976), xix.

131 The epigraph attributed to Herman Daly is from his book *Beyond Growth* (Boston, Beacon Press, 1994), 11.

131–132 Accounts of native peoples' attitudes toward material wealth are given by Marshall Sahlins, "The Sadness of Sweetness," *Current Anthropology* 37, no. 3 (1996): 395–428; Elman Service, *Profiles in Ethnology* (New York: Harper and Row, 1963); and David Suzuki and Peter Knudtson, *Wisdom of the Elders* (New York: Bantam Books, 1993).

132 A classic account of the effect of markets on traditional societies is Karl Polanyi, *The Great Transformation* (Boston: Beacon Press, 1944). See also Robert Heilbroner, *21st Century Capitalism* (New York: Norton, 1994).

132–133 Western influence on Nauru is discussed by Camilla H. Wedgwood, "Report on Research Work on Nauru Island, Central Pacific (part one)," *Oceania* 6 (1936a): 359–94; and Camilla H. Wedgwood, "Report on Research Work on Nauru Island, Central Pacific (part two)," *Oceania* 7 (1936b): 1–33.

132–135 The introduction of the market economy to the Nauruans is documented by Nancy Viviani, *Nauru: Phosphate and Political Progress* (Canberra: Australian National University Press, 1970); Maslyn Williams and Barrie Macdonald, *The Phosphateers* (Melbourne: Melbourne University Press, 1985); and Christopher Weeramantry, *Nauru: Environmental Damage under International Trusteeship* (Melbourne: Oxford University Press, 1992).

135 The description of the ravages of World War II come from several

diaries from Ocean Island (Banaba) and Nauru Island available from Gaston Renard, G.P.O. 5235BB, Melbourne, Victoria 3001, Australia: Ocean Island [From what I have Heard, Read and seen], Anonymous, dated March 1946; Report on the Japanese Occupation of Ocean Island, Bauro Ratieta, dated January 1944; Interrogation of Morning Star — 21st January 1945; Interrogation of Nabetari, dated "about March 1945"; Interrogation of Kabunare, dated December 1945; Nauru [Mainly from What I Saw], Anonymous, dated 8th March 1946; The War Diary of D. Patrick Cook [a native Nauruan] commencing 8th December 1940 and ending 9th August 1945. Recently published accounts can be found in Jemima Garrett, *Island Exiles* (Sydney: ABC Books, 1996).

137 The resistance of indigenous peoples to colonialism is discussed by Marshall Sahlins, *How Natives Think* (Chicago: University of Chicago Press, 1995).

138–139 The cost of economic growth is discussed by E. J. Mishan, *The Costs of Economic Growth* (New York: Praeger, 1967); Nicholas Georgescu-Roegen, *The Entropy Law and the Economic Process* (Cambridge: Harvard University Press, 1971); Herman Daly and John Cobb, *For the Common Good* (Boston: Beacon Press, 1989); R. Douthwaite, *The Cost of Economic Growth* (Tulsa, Okla.: Council Oak Books, 1992); and Robert Kutner, *Everything for Sale* (New York: Knopf, 1998).

140–142 Discussions of weak sustainability can be found in R. Solow, "Sustainability: An Economist's Perspective," in *Economics of the Environment,* 3d ed., ed. R. Dorfman and N. Dorfman (New York: W. W. Norton, 1991); D. Pearce and G. Atkinson, "Capital Theory and the Measurement of Sustainable Development: An Indicator of 'Weak Sustainability,'" *Ecological Economics* 8 (1993): 103–8; J. Gowdy and S. O'Hara, "Weak Sustainability and Viable Technologies," *Ecological Economics* 22 (1997): 239–48; and Daniel Bromley, "Searching for Sustainability: The Poverty of Spontaneous Order," *Ecological Economics* 24 (1998): 231–40. Nauru as an example of weak sustainability is discussed by J. Gowdy and C. McDaniel, "The Physical Destruction of Nauru: An Example of Weak Sustainability," *Land Economics* 75 (1999): 333–38.

142–143 Strong sustainability is discussed by Robert Goodland, Herman Daly, and Salah El Serafy, "The Urgent Need for Rapid Transition to Global Environmental Sustainability," *Environmental Conservation* 20 (1993):

297–309; and Daly and Cobb (1989). See also Yvonne Baskin, *The Work of Nature* (Washington, D.C.: Island Press, 1997); Gretchen Daily, ed., *Nature's Services* (Washington, D.C.: Island Press, 1997); and Paul Ehrlich, *A World of Wounds: Ecologists and the Human Dilemma* (Oldendorf/Luhe: Ecology Institute, 1997).

143   Criticisms of the maximum sustainable yield policy can be found in D. Ludwig, R. Hilborn, and C. Walters, "Uncertainty, Resource Exploitation, and Conservation: Lessons from History," *Science* 260 (1993): 17, 36; Susan Hanna, "The New Frontier in Fisheries Governance," *Ecological Economics* 20 (1995): 221–33; and Daniel Pauly et al., "Fishing down Marine Food Webs," *Science* 279 (1998): 860–63.

143–144 Discussions of the workings of market economies are given by D. Pearce and K. Turner, *Economics of Natural Resources and the Environment* (Baltimore: Johns Hopkins University Press, 1990); J. Gowdy and C. McDaniel, "One World, One Experiment: Addressing the Biodiversity-Economics Conflict," *Ecological Economics* 14 (1995): 180–92; J. Gowdy and S. O'Hara, *Economic Theory for Environmentalists* (Delray Beach, Fla.: St. Lucie Press, 1995).

144–145 An excellent discussion of discounting is presented by C. Price, *Time, Discounting and Value* (Cambridge, Mass.: Basil Blackwell, 1993). See also J. Gowdy, "Society and Ecosystems: Discounting and the Social Aspects of Biodiversity Protection," *International Journal of Social Economics* 23 (1996): 49–63.

146   The figures for the prices of animal parts are given in A. Gordon and D. Suzuki, *A Matter of Survival* (Sydney: Allen and Unwin, 1990).

146–148 Case studies of markets and biodiversity loss are found in A. Schorger, *The Passenger Pigeon* (Norman: University of Oklahoma Press, 1973); C. Safina, "Bluefin Tuna in the West Atlantic: Negligent Management and the Making of an Endangered Species," *Conservation Biology* 7 (1993): 229–34; and Carl McDaniel and John Gowdy, "Markets and Biodiversity Loss: Some Case Studies and Policy Considerations," *International Journal of Social Economics* 25, no. 10 (1998): 1454–65.

149   The Stephen Jay Gould quotation is from "The Golden Rule—a Proper Scale for Our Environmental Crisis," *Natural History* (September 1990): 24–30.

150–154 The stories of Mangaia and Tikopia are found in Raymond Firth, *The*

Work of the Gods in Tikopia (New York: Humanities Press, 1967); Patrick Kirch, "Changing Landscapes and Sociopolitical Evolution in Mangaia, Central Polynesia," in *Historical Ecology in the Pacific Islands: Prehistoric Environmental and Landscape Changes*, ed. Patrick V. Kirch and Terry L. Hunt (New Haven: Yale University Press, 1997); and Patrick Kirch, "Microcosmic Histories, Island Perspectives on 'Global' Change," *American Anthropologist* 99 (1997): 30–42.

153–154   The Kirch quotation is from Patrick Kirch (1997).

154   References and discussion of twentieth-century environmental history can be found in Donald Worster, *Nature's Economy* (Cambridge: Cambridge University Press, 1977); and Donald Worster, *The Wealth of Nature: Environmental History and the Ecological Imagination* (New York: Oxford University Press, 1993). See also various publications of the Worldwatch Institute.

Chapter Eight. The Chimera of Reality

156   The epigraph is from Aldo Leopold, *A Sand County Almanac and Sketches Here and There* (Oxford: Oxford University Press, 1949), viii, 209–10.

157   The quotation on the opinion of the Nauruan Council is from Nancy Viviani, *Nauru: Phosphate and Political Progress* (Canberra: Australian National University Press, 1970), 164; and the quotation expressing Australian attitudes is from *Canberra Times*, February 1966, in Viviani (1970), 156.

157   Australian dollar values of phosphate are calculated from data in Viviani (1970).

160–161   James Aingimea is quoted in "A Pacific Island Nation Is Stripped of Everything," *New York Times* (Internet service), December 10, 1995.

161   The first quotation giving the Western outlook is from an editor of a respected regional publication, quoted by Jack Anderson, a syndicated columnist, in the *Troy (New York) Record*, July 9, 1997; the second quotation, which expresses a similar viewpoint, is from a Western diplomat, quoted in Dale Van Atta, "Paradise Squandered," *Reader's Digest* (May 1997): 88.

162   The biological effects of hormone mimics are discussed in Theo

Colborn, Dianne Dumanoski, John Peterson Myers, *Our Stolen Future* (New York: Penguin Group, 1996).

164 The quotation about Australian aborigines is from David Suzuki and Peter Knudtson, *Wisdom of the Elders* (New York: Bantam Books, 1992), 46.

166 World Energy Council numbers for energy use can be found in Edward Carr, "Energy: The New Prize," *The Economist* (June 18, 1994): 3–18.

166 A discussion of the subsidies for fossil fuels can be found in Harold M. Hubbard, "The Real Cost of Energy," *Scientific American* 264 (April 1991): 36–42.

168 Using conservative estimates, Dr. David Borton — president, Sustainable Energy Systems, Troy, New York — has calculated the fraction of the world's deserts needed to produce all the energy currently used in the world by means of current solar trough technology. The number of btus produced per hectare (ha) is 3×10^9 btu — (1 ha $\times 10^4$ m^2/ha $\times 0.25$ [fraction of land covered by collectors] $\times 0.20$ [solar efficiency of energy conversion] $\times 1 kW/m^2 \times 2000$ hrs/yr $\times 3400$ btu/kW hr $= 3 \times 10^9$ btu). The world currently uses about 360 Quads of energy (one Quad equals 10^{15} btu), and it would therefore take 120×10^6 hectares of desert to provide 360 Quads (360 Q $\div 3 \times 10^9$ btu/ha $= 120 \times 10^6$ ha). The desert area of the world is about 1.5×10^9 ha, and 120×10^6 ha is less than 10 percent of this area.

168 Wind power in the Midwest is discussed by the Union of Concerned Scientists, *Powering the Midwest* (Boston: Union of Concerned Scientists, 1993).

168 For running the world on solar energy and using less energy, see Christopher Flavin and Nicholas Lenssen, *Power Surge: Guide to the Coming Energy Revolution* (New York: Norton, 1994); Ross Gelbspan, *The Heat Is ON* (New York: Addison-Wesley, 1997); Ged R. Davis, "Energy for Planet Earth," *Scientific American* 263 (September 1990): 54–62; Carl J. Weinberg and Robert H. Williams, "Energy from the Sun," *Scientific American* 263 (September 1990): 146–55; and John P. Holdren, "Energy in Transition," *Scientific American* 263 (September 1990): 156–63.

168–169 The amount of ecologically productive land required to support different lifestyles is given in Mathis Wackernagel and William Rees, *Our Ecological Footprint* (Gabriola Island: New Society Publishers, 1996).

169   Issues of consumption and lifestyles are discussed in Alan Durning, *How Much Is Enough?* (New York: Norton, 1992).

169–170   Trade among Henderson, Pitcairn, and Mangareva is discussed by Jared Diamond, "Paradises Lost," *Discover Magazine* (November 1997): 69–78.

170–171   Tikopia is discussed by Patrick Kirch, "Microcosmic Histories, Island Perspectives on 'Global' Change," *American Anthropologist* 99 (1997): 30–42.

171–174   How to change to create a durable world civilization is an immense challenge. A thoughtful and realistic discussion of this challenge is found in Kai N. Lee, *Compass and Gyroscope* (Washington, D.C.: Island Press, 1993).

Index

Designer: Nola Burger
Compositor: BookMatters
Text: 11/15 Granjon
Display: Texas Hero
Printer and binder: Haddon Craftsmen, Inc.